SPEAKING ABOUT WHAT WE HAVE SEEN AND HEARD

SPEAKING ABOUT WHAT WE HAVE SEEN AND HEARD

Evangelism in Global Perspective

Edited by

Jonathan J. Bonk
Dwight P. Baker
Daniel J. Nicholas
Craig A. Noll

OMSC Publications
New Haven, Connecticut

Published by OMSC Publications
Overseas Ministries Study Center
490 Prospect Street
New Haven, CT 06511 USA
(203) 624-6672   www.OMSC.org

For information on the INTERNATIONAL BULLETIN OF MISSIONARY RESEARCH, visit www.InternationalBulletin.org or www.OMSC.org.

Front cover: *The Plentiful Harvest,* by Sawai Chinnawong, from *Christ on the Bangkok Road: The Art of Sawai Chinnawong* (OMSC Publications, 2007).

ISBN: 0-9762205-4-7
Printed in the United States of America

Contents

Contributors

David B. Barrett, an *IBMR* contributing editor, is editor of the *World Christian Encyclopedia: A Comparative Study of Churches and Religions in the Modern World*, A.D. *1900–2000* (1982), coauthor of the second edition (2001), and author of *Schism and Renewal in Africa: An Analysis of Six Thousand Contemporary Religious Movements* (1968). He is founder of the World Evangelization Research Centre, Richmond, Virginia.

Jonathan J. Bonk is executive director of the Overseas Ministries Study Center, New Haven, Connecticut, and editor of the INTERNATIONAL BULLETIN OF MISSIONARY RESEARCH. He is also project director for the *Dictionary of African Christian Biography*—a multilingual, electronic, nonproprietary reference tool—and author of *Missions and Money: Affluence as a Missionary Problem . . . Revisited* (2006). Bonk was professor of global Christian studies, Providence College and Seminary, in Canada.

Kenneth Cragg, a major figure in the field of Christian-Muslim dialogue, spent some forty-five years in the Middle East as a professor of philosophy, as a chaplain, and as assistant bishop in the Anglican Archdiocese of Jerusalem. He has also taught at the University of Sussex in England. Among his many books are *The Qur'an and the West* (2006) and *The Call of the Minaret* (1956).

Peter F. Crossing is an Australian missiologist, a database programmer, and an editorial associate for the second edition of the *World Christian Encyclopedia* (2001). Formerly information coordinator at the Sydney Centre for World Mission, Crossing interprets and disseminates the results of missiological research to churches and mission agencies. He also provides database consulting for the National Church Life Survey and data analysis with MapInfo Australia.

Paul A. Eshleman, a staff member of Campus Crusade for Christ, directed the 1976 "I Found It" evangelistic outreach to cities across the United States. He was U.S. field director for Campus Crusade for Christ until being seconded in 1976 to the Genesis Project. Since 1981 he has directed the Jesus Film Project of Campus Crusade for Christ.

Philip Jenkins, author of *The Next Christendom: The Coming of Global Christianity* (2002), is distinguished professor of history and religious studies at Pennsylvania State University, University Park, Pennsylvania. *The Next Christendom* won the 2003 *Christianity Today* Book Award for the best book in the category of "Christianity and Culture." An *IBMR* contributing editor, he is also author of *The New Faces of Christianity: Believing the Bible in the Global South* (2006).

Todd M. Johnson is director of the Center for the Study of Global Christianity, at Gordon-Conwell Theological Seminary, South Hamilton, Massachusetts, and coauthor of the *World Christian Encyclopedia* (2nd edition, 2001). He was director of the World Evangelization Research Center, Richmond, Virginia, and is co-founder of the Christian Futures Network, a member of the World Future Society.

David A. Kerr is chair of missiology and ecumenics at the Centre for Theology and Religious Studies, Lund University, Sweden. An *IBMR* contributing editor, previously he was professor and director of the Centre for the Study of Christianity in the Non-Western World at the University of Edinburgh and director of the Duncan Black Macdonald Center for the Study of Islam and Christian-Muslim Relations, at Hartford Seminary, Hartford, Connecticut.

Alan Kreider is associate professor of church history and mission at Associated Mennonite Biblical Seminary, Elkhart, Indiana. For twenty-six years he was a missionary in England with the Mennonite Board of Missions. He is author of *The Change of Conversion and the Origin of Christendom* (1999) and editor of *The Origins of Christendom in the West* (2001).

Richard V. Peace is professor of evangelism and spiritual formation in the School of Theology at Fuller Theological Seminary, Pasadena, California. He was professor of evangelism and ministry and director of media education at Gordon-Conwell Theological Seminary in South Hamilton, Massachusetts. He is author of *Conversion in the New Testament: Paul and the Twelve* (1999) and *Pilgrimage: A Handbook on Christian Growth* (1984).

Wilbert R. Shenk is senior professor of mission history and contemporary culture at Fuller Theological Seminary, Pasadena, California. Previously he was a missionary in Indonesia, a mission administrator, and director of the Mission Training Center at Associated Mennonite Biblical Seminaries, Elkhart, Indiana. An *IBMR* contributing editor, he is editor of *North American Foreign Missions, 1810–1914: Theology, Theory, and Policy* (2004).

Timothy C. Tennent is professor of world missions and Indian studies and director of missions programs at Gordon-Conwell Theological Seminary, South Hamilton, Massachusetts. He is also an adjunct professor at the Luther W. New, Jr. Theological College, Dehra Dun, India, where he has traveled annually since 1988. Tennent is author of *Christianity at the Religious Roundtable: Evangelicals in Conversation with Hinduism, Buddhism, and Islam* (2002).

Andrew F. Walls, a former missionary in Sierra Leone and Nigeria, was director of the Centre for the Study of Christianity in the Non-Western World, at the University of Edinburgh. An *IBMR* contributing editor, he is honorary professor in the Universities of Edinburgh and Aberdeen. He is author of *The Missionary Movement in Christian History: Studies in the Transmission of Faith* (1996) and *The Cross-cultural Process in Christian History* (2002).

Christopher J. H. Wright is international director of Langham Partnership International, London, a network of ministries known in the United States as John Stott Ministries. Previously he taught Old Testament courses at Union Biblical Seminary, Pune, India, and was principal of All Nations Christian College, in Hertfordshire, England. He is author of *The Mission of God: Unlocking the Bible's Grand Narrative* (2006) and *Old Testament Ethics for the People of God* (2004).

Preface

"Just what *is* the Gospel?" This deceptively simple question was posed on the masthead of the January 2006 issue of the INTERNATIONAL BULLETIN OF MISSIONARY RESEARCH. The question has led to a confusing range of responses across time and cultures by those who have embraced the Good News—namely, through Jesus Christ human beings, and indeed all of creation, can be reconciled to God.

At the heart of Christianity is the "Gospel"—from Old English *gōdspel*, "glad tidings, good news," which directly translates the Greek *euangelion*. Since the *IBMR*, in which the chapters in this book first appeared, is devoted to the study of Christian mission, it is not surprising that "Gospel" and its cognates have been among its most frequently recurring themes. A simple keyword search for "Gospel" in the ATLAS (American Theological Library Association Serials) online version of the *IBMR* (1981–2004) yielded seventy-three entries. Another fifty articles were flagged by the word "evangelism," while "evangelization" produced a list of forty-eight separate articles.

Just *what* is the Gospel? The Nicene Creed—crafted in 325 C.E. and fine-tuned by the Council of Constantinople in 381—encapsulates the core beliefs of most Orthodox, Roman Catholics, and Protestants. Few Christian groups would demur from its distilled doctrines. But does such an elegantly crafted creed, even if it is a kind of epistemological vertebra of Christianity, constitute the "Gospel"? Or does one find the Gospel's quintessential expression in the record of our Lord's life and the Sermon on the Mount—his Kingdom charter? While the Gospel is both of these, and more, the unique imprint of our own culture and personal experience deeply influence both our understanding and our proclamation of the Good News.

Who decides whether the Gospel is good news? Jesus was impelled by "the Spirit of the Lord . . . to bring good news to the poor" (Luke 4:18). Given our human bent for fashioning one-size-fits-all religious templates in witnessing to the Gospel, our Lord's willingness to bring good news to people on *their* terms—restoration of withered limbs, sight for sightless eyes, rejuvenation of dying or already deceased loved ones, exorcism of demons, wine for a party, mercy for an adulteress, healing for leprous bodies, food for the hungry, and public rebuke of hypocritical religious bigots—is instructive.

Those whose lives were transformed by such good news were understandably spontaneous in their proclamation of the good news of their encounters with Jesus. Take, for example, the story recorded in John 9. Who or where Jesus might be, the man who had been sightless from birth could not tell. "One thing I do know," he told his exasperated interrogators, "that though I was blind, now I see" (v. 25). Appalled by any suggestion that Jesus might be more than a charlatan, the religious leaders had earlier quizzed the man's mother and father. Etched into their parental memories would have been their helpless anguish at the plight of their infant son, and their aching efforts to see him survive with dignity in a society where begging would likely be his only option. These parents—numb with shock—could only confirm their son's identity and affirm his inexplicable transformation: "We know that this is our son, and that he was born blind; but we do not know how it is that now he sees, nor do we know who opened his eyes" (vv. 20–21).

That such good news should be kept under wraps was inconceivable then, and it has been impossible ever since. Sternly prohibited from proclaiming the Gospel of the risen Lord, Peter and John responded, "We cannot keep from speaking about what we have seen and heard" (Acts 4:20).

Each of the eleven essays in this volume provides some insight into Christian proclamation of the Good News that Jesus the Christ, who both engages and transcends human time and culture, freely offers to liberate the deepest potential of persons, families, and communities so that God's kingdom can come and God's will can be done on earth as it is in heaven. In bringing these essays together into a single, accessible source, the editors' hope is modestly to serve this cause célèbre.

—Jonathan J. Bonk
November 2007

Acknowledgments

All of the chapters in this volume originally appeared in the pages of the INTERNATIONAL BULLETIN OF MISSIONARY RESEARCH *(www.InternationalBulletin.org).*

David B. Barrett, Todd M. Johnson, and Peter F. Crossing, "Missiometrics 2006: Goals, Resources, Doctrines of the 350 Christian World Communions," *IBMR* 30, no. 1 (January 2006): 27–30.

Kenneth Cragg, "Prepositions and Salvation," *IBMR* 17, no. 1 (January 1993): 2–3.

Paul A. Eshleman, "The 'Jesus' Film: A Contribution to World Evangelism," *IBMR* 26, no. 2 (April 2002): 68–72.

Philip Jenkins, "Reading the Bible in the Global South," *IBMR* 28, no. 1 (January 2004): 20–22.

David A. Kerr, "Mission and Proselytism: A Middle East Perspective," *IBMR* 20, no. 1 (January 1996): 12–22.

Alan Kreider, "Beyond Bosch: The Early Church and the Christendom Shift," *IBMR* 29, no. 2 (April 2005): 59–68.

Richard V. Peace, "Conflicting Understandings of Christian Conversion: A Missiological Challenge," *IBMR* 28, no. 1 (January 2004): 8–14.

Wilbert R. Shenk, "New Wineskins for New Wine: Toward a Post-Christendom Ecclesiology," *IBMR* 29, no. 2 (April 2005): 73–79.

Timothy C. Tennent, "The Challenge of Churchless Christianity: An Evangelical Assessment," *IBMR* 29, no. 4 (October 2005): 171–77.

Andrew F. Walls, "Converts or Proselytes? The Crisis over Conversion in the Early Church," *IBMR* 28, no. 1 (January 2004): 2–6.

Christopher J. H. Wright, "Implications of Conversion in the Old Testament and the New," *IBMR* 28, no. 1 (January 2004): 14–19.

1

Converts or Proselytes? The Crisis over Conversion in the Early Church

Andrew F. Walls

The word *conversion* has been used in Christian history in a multitude of ways. There have been at least two broad streams of usage, each with many divisions. In one stream conversion is spoken of essentially as an external act of religious change. In this usage Christian conversion refers to movement to the Christian faith, individually or collectively, on the part of people previously outside it. By extension, this usage can also indicate movement from one branch of Christian profession to another—from Catholic to Protestant, for instance, or vice versa.

In the second stream of usage, "conversion" denotes critical internal religious change in persons within the Christian community, and here the varieties of meaning raise complex issues. Sometimes "conversion" refers to subjective experience, sometimes to an assumed ontological change, sometimes to both. For centuries in the Latin West, the primary meaning of "conversion" was a person's response to vocation to the religious or monastic life, turning from the life of the world to God. In Protestant devotion it came to refer to an early stage of the pilgrimage of the soul awakened to God. Catholics, Jansenists, mainstream Protestants, radical Protestants, Puritans, Pietists, and Arminian and Calvinist evangelicals developed differing maps of the processes of salvation and differing paradigms of "normal" Christian experience. These in turn led to different assessments of the nature and significance of conversion and of its relationship to regeneration, justification, and other elements in the salvific process. They also raised the question whether conversion was always necessary where Christian nurture had been effective. New styles of evangelism, with new understandings of the saving process, that developed in the nineteenth and twentieth centuries complicated matters further. Whole new vocabularies of evangelism came into existence, and the word "conversion" had a place in all of them. Where the vital question is "Are you saved?" or "Have you accepted Jesus into

1

your heart?" "conversion" is likely to mean something rather different from what it means when the question is, "How long have you been at Sinai, and what is your law work?" as it might be in the older Scottish evangelicalism, or "Have you the form of godliness, and do you desire the power thereof?" which might be raised if an inquirer sought membership of an early Methodist society.

The Protestant missionary movement complicated the understanding of conversion still further. Missions aimed to bring into the Christian faith those who were outside it, but those who were most active in establishing missions were often evangelicals, who had a well-defined paradigm of "normal" Christian experience. The evangelical conversion they had experienced had taken them from the "nominal" Christianity professed throughout the society in which they had grown up to "real" Christianity issuing in a holy life. This process was typically marked by a period of deep consciousness of personal sin followed by a sense of joyous liberation dawning with realization of personal forgiveness through Christ. Missionaries with this background expected to see a similar pattern of experience in those who came to Christian faith, even in societies where there had been no previous Christian profession. In this way, the distinction between the two streams of usage—the one relating to externally recognizable adhesion to the Christian faith and the other relating to internal personal change—became blurred. This was not the first time that such blurring occurred. There had long been confusion within the first stream of usage when referring to such celebrated conversions as those of Constantine and Augustine, where "conversion" might be used equally of their identification (in their different ways) with the Christian community, or of the particular critical experiences that led them to it.

This essay does not attempt to disentangle these linguistic and conceptual complexities. It seeks to focus on the simplest, most elemental feature of the word "conversion," the idea of turning. There is ample biblical warrant for this focus in the insistence with which the Scriptures of both testaments call for turning to God. One might almost say that conversion represents the specifically Christian understanding of the response to God's saving activity. The events that best illuminate our understanding of it are described in the New Testament.

The Jewishness of the Early Church

The earliest church, as we meet it in the early chapters of the Acts of the Apostles, was utterly Jewish. It was made up, virtually without exception, of people of Jewish birth and inheritance. They met every day in the temple (Acts 2:46), where they regularly attended "the prayers" (Acts 2:42), that is, the temple liturgy, thus congregating in a place where (beyond an outer court) none but Jews could go. Presiding over the church was James, the brother of Jesus, a man nicknamed "The Righteous" by his neighbors, who recognized that he was righteous in the Jewish sense of heartfelt obedience to the law. Whatever the differences among them in background and language—and that there were such differences, and that they had theological aspects, is clear from the record—they all saw Jesus and his work from the perspective of Israel's history, hopes, and expectations. Their priorities and concerns are thoroughly Jewish: as the disillusioned disciple on the way to Emmaus says, they had seen Jesus as the one who would set Israel free (Luke 24:21). On the mount of ascension the preoccupation is the same. Realizing that they are standing at the threshold of a new era, the disciples ask the Lord if he is now about to give the kingdom back to Israel (Acts 1:6). They cannot conceive of Jesus' saving work without its political climax in the history of Israel because, in Jewish terms, salvation is unintelligible without the salvation of the nation. Nor does Jesus deny this idea or tell them they have misunderstood his mission; he simply tells them that the times and seasons are in the Father's hands (Acts 1:7).

There were, of course, things that marked out the company of Jesus believers from all other varieties of observant Jew. What outsiders would probably notice first was a distinctive lifestyle among these Jesus people. They shared property, making special provision for vulnerable sectors of the community such as widows. And they had frequent communal meals, eating in one another's houses (Acts 2:44–46). In the sphere of belief, their most distinctive feature was their identification of three key figures in the Scriptures of Israel—the Davidic Messiah who was the national savior, the Son of Man who would figure in the judgment of the world, and the Suffering Servant who sacrificed himself for his people—with the recent prophet and teacher Jesus of Nazareth. Jesus was universally known to have been put to death by the Romans, but the community vigorously asserted that he had risen from the dead.

None of these things, however, meant that these people had taken on a new religion. Rather, these beliefs gave them deep insight into, and deeper understanding of, the religion they had always had. They did not even know that they were Christians; the word had not yet been coined (Acts 11:26). They needed no special name; they were Israel. They had not less reverence for the Torah than before, but more; they remembered that Jesus had said that not the smallest letter of the law would be lost by his agency. They had not less reverence for the temple, but more, for they remembered how Jesus had cleansed it and called it his Father's house, recalling the old scripture about the zeal of God's house consuming his chosen one (John 2:17). They saw no reason to cease animal sacrifices; in the light of the Suffering Servant's self-offering, they understood them better. Their favorite title for Jesus, Messiah, was steeped in the history of Israel and in convictions about Israel's destiny. Jesus made sense of Jewish history; everything about him made sense in Jewish terms.

This did not mean, however, that the Jesus community accepted the life of the Israel of that day. On the contrary, their preaching, as it is described in Acts, carries the note of crisis, a repeated call for decision. A new age had arrived; it was time for Israel to turn from the old ways (Acts 2:28–30).

This note of crisis, focused on the call to turn, was not new. It was one of the dominating themes of the Scriptures of Israel. The root *shubh* occurs in the Hebrew Bible no less than 750 times with the sense of turning, or (in a causative form, with God as agent) in the sense of being turned, brought back, or restored. These uses are especially characteristic of the prophetic Scriptures. These often show Israel worshiping gods other than Yahweh, setting up a society marked by opulence, extortion, injustice, and oppression of the poor, giving Israel's God a bad name among foreign nations (Isa. 2:6–18; 5:6–13, Ezek. 36:22). The consequences are defeat, occupation, and exile (Isa.1:1–9). But the same Scriptures use that same language of turning to show a process whereby God "turns the nation back" and restores it, rescuing the defeated nation, bringing back the exiles, and receiving the praise of a righteous, redeemed people (Isa. 51:11). Indeed, even when apostasy is rife, there is a "righteous remnant" that is the nucleus of the true Israel (Isa. 8:16–18; 10:20–22). The Messiah, the personal agent of God in restoring Israel, reigns forever over the restored nation with a rule that is unfailingly just and equitable (Isa. 11:1–5). Moral renewal follows inner transformation: people will adhere to God from their hearts (Jer. 31:31–34). And this change will herald universal renewal, in which the flora and fauna and the whole environment are enriched and violence is unknown, and the Gentiles will acknowledge Yahweh as their own God (Isa. 11:6–9). The messianic age will bless the whole world. The recurrent call of the prophets is for Israel to turn to face the age to come; that is, the call to conversion.

Such is the framework within which that earliest church did its thinking. We see the framework even in the Synoptic Gospels. The focus of the Messiah's work is the renewal of Israel. (The angel tells

Joseph to name the child Jesus because he will save his people—that is, Israel—from their sins, Matt. 1:21.) The story of the ministry of Jesus has as a preface an account of John the Baptist—indeed, Mark even calls John's ministry "the beginning of the Gospel" (Mark 1:1). The ministry of John, like that of the earlier prophets, is a call for turning—for conversion. He calls for radical change of mind ("repentance") in the light of the establishment of God's personal rule ("the kingdom of God," see Matt. 3:1–11). And the change of mind is symbolized in the rite that gave "John the Dipper" his nickname. Almost certainly John did not invent baptism. Something like it was already in use as a purification rite at the initiation of Gentiles who wished to enter Israel. It was a symbolic washing away of the filth of the heathen world. John's revolution was to require the baptism of Jews; the covenant people, according to the preaching of John, needed cleansing as much as did any idolatrous Gentile. Jews who sought John's baptism implicitly recognized their moral equivalence with Gentile outsiders.

The early chapters of Acts depict a community whose original members would have received John's baptism, and whose whole education prepared them for the arrival of the messianic age, and with it the restoration and renewal of Israel. The community proclaims the arrival of the Messiah, and those who so recognize Jesus accept baptism, thus acknowledging their need for change of mind, and "receive the gift of the Holy Spirit" (Acts 2:38–39). In the prophetic writings the Spirit of God indicates a divine activity particularly marking the messianic age (Joel 2:28–32). Believers undergo a radical change of lifestyle; they share their property, share their meals, and give careful attention to marginalized people (Acts 2:43–45; 4:32–35; 6:1–4). In doing so, they turn away from the exploitative ways so often characteristic of the life of Israel, the things that the prophets had denounced. This is the messianic community, the community that has morally turned, a righteous community. Here is the evidence that the restoration of Israel has begun. Jesus is saving his people Israel, heirs of the prophetic promises and of the covenant, from their sins (Acts 3:24–26).

This church is completely Jewish in composition and thinking, Jewish at the very roots of its identity. There is no sign of their going into all the world to preach the Gospel to every creature. The few people who joined the community from outside Israel—the family of Cornelius, the Samaritans, the Ethiopian eunuch—came, not through some evangelistic policy, but through what one might call divine or providential nudges; and all, even if not accepted as Israelites, were already worshipers of Israel's God. In the church of the early chapters of Acts, the traditional institutions of Israel—Torah, temple, sacrificial cultus—keep their ancient place. That church made a profound impact on its society, so that many thousands of zealous Torah-keeping Jews came forward to share in the messianic restoration of Israel and share in the times of refreshing that the restoration brings (Acts 3:19–20). But even as servants of Messiah Jesus, they were still zealous for the Torah (Acts 21:20).

This is Jewish life and Jewish thought—but it is Jewish life and thought converted. It is life lived, and thinking done, in terms of the messianic age, long spoken of as the Age to Come, and now arrived: inaugurated by the Messiah, just as the prophets had said would happen. This is Jewish life and thought turned toward Messiah Jesus.

Disruption and Change

Left to themselves, the earliest church members might have continued to demonstrate the messianic renewal and restoration of Israel, sharing in the apostles' teaching and fellowship, breaking social bread together, and attending the temple liturgy (Acts 2:42) until Jerusalem fell about their ears. But they were not left to themselves. What happened was no part of deliberate church strategy, and the people responsible for it were not apostles or leading figures in the church. We do not even know their names. Nevertheless the events mark a turning point in Christian history. It seems to have begun with Stephen's explosive preaching and the disturbance that followed it and led to his death. Many believers were forced out of Jerusalem; it would be natural for them to seek shelter in the Jewish communities beyond Israel (Acts 6:8–8:1). Most of them did what they had done in Jerusalem and proclaimed Jesus as Messiah in the Jewish communities (Acts 11:19). But some people (it is remarked that they were of Cypriot and Libyan background), arriving in the cosmopolitan city of Antioch, began to talk about Jesus to "Greeks"—that is, to pagans (Acts 11:20).

This meant talking about Jesus in a new way. There was little to be gained by stressing the ethnic term "Messiah." It could be translated into Greek easily enough, but the translation ("the Smeared One") would still seem odd to anyone not well acquainted with Jewish institutions. Explaining it would require a lengthy introduction to the Scriptures; and supposing there were Greek pagans with the interest and stamina to pay attention, they might still be puzzled to see any relevance to their own situation. Why should they rejoice that the national savior of Israel had arrived? What sort of good news to them was the restoration of Israel?

The believers from Cyprus and Cyrene, although for them person-
ally the messiahship of Jesus must have seemed the key to the Gospel,
took a different route. Linguistic translation was not enough; conceptual
translation was necessary in order to convey the fact that Jesus had
ultimate significance for Greek pagans, just as he had for devout Jews.
They presented Jesus as Lord, *Kyrios*. It was a word that Jews could use
readily enough of the Messiah; Peter speaks to a Jewish audience of Jesus being made "both Lord and Messiah" (Acts 2:36). But the believers
must have known that in Antioch "Lord" was the title of cult divinities
like Sarapis. And perhaps by this means Greek pagans could get their
first inkling of who Jesus is by hearing of him as the divine lord, *Kyrios
Iesous*, just as other devotees addressed *Kyrios Sarapis*.

This piece of cross-cultural communication was soon reinforced by
a decision of permanent significance for the Christian faith. As people
of Greek and pagan background responded to this presentation of Jesus
in Antioch and far beyond it (for Antioch, rather than Jerusalem, turned
out to be the missionary church), the status of those who responded
had to be considered. And at the so-called Apostolic Council described
in Acts 15, the apostles and elders at Jerusalem, themselves pious,
law-keeping people under the presidency of James, the outstandingly
law-righteous brother of the Lord, agreed that followers of Jesus the
Messiah, even if not ethnic Jews, had indeed entered Israel. They did
not need the traditional signs of Jewish religious culture, circumcision
and Torah-keeping.

To explore the significance of the decision, we should remember
Israel's long missionary tradition whereby Gentile proselytes had been
welcomed to the fold of Israel. Rabbinic literature compared them to
stags, whose natural habitat was in the wild, grazing with sheep of the
flock. Synagogues in the dispersion often had numbers of such people,
and the later chapters of Acts suggest that they were fertile soil for the
preaching of Paul and other missionaries (Acts 13:48; 17:4). Israel had
long known of people like David's Moabite ancestor Ruth, who declared
that their people would be Israel, and their God Israel's God (Ruth
1:16). But a Gentile male needed to undergo circumcision, receiving
the mark of the covenant with God, as the sign of adoption into Israel.
Later the further requirement of baptism gave additional solemnity to
the transition of the proselyte from the heathen world of the nations to
the life of the Nation.

Furthermore, several passages in the prophetic writings indicated
that the messianic age would see floods of Gentiles seeking the God of
Israel. Thus in Isaiah 2 and Micah 4 many peoples will decide to go up to

the mountain of the Lord, to the house of the God of Jacob. In Zechariah ten men from all languages and nations will take firm hold of one Jew by the edge of his robe and go with him because they have heard that God is with him (Zech. 8:23). So as Jerusalem believers listened to the reports of the missionaries of the Antiochene church, they would receive a yet higher sense of confirmation that the promised messianic age had arrived. But these same Scriptures talked of the word of the Lord going out from Zion (Isa. 2:3) and of "the mountain of the Lord's house," that is, the hill on which the temple stood, being established as the principal mountain (Isa. 2:2). Perhaps it is not surprising that many Jerusalem believers took it for granted that the believing Greeks in Antioch and beyond should be treated as enlightened Gentiles had always been treated in Israel. They were proselytes, stags that had chosen to graze with the sheep. In addition to the baptism they had received (and there was in any case an established custom of baptizing proselytes), they should be circumcised and, being thus incorporated into Israel, keep the Torah as good Israelites. After all, the Torah was Israel's most precious possession, given by God himself and marking Israel out from other nations—should not all followers of Israel's Messiah keep and cherish it? And what greater gift or blessing could these newly adopted Israelites receive? If circumcision was the mark of the covenant, should not those newly brought within the covenant carry that mark? The only way of life known to the earliest believers in Jesus—the only known Christian lifestyle, to use an anachronism—was that of pious, observant Jews. It was the way of life sanctified by the Messiah himself, maintained by his closest disciples (Peter had never eaten anything common or unclean), and outstandingly patterned by the brother who had grown up in the same home as the Messiah.

It is not surprising that many Jerusalem believers evidently thought on these lines. Nor is it too surprising that numbers of new Gentile believers were ready to go along with the argument. Some of them had doubtless attended the synagogue for many years, convinced that Israel's God was indeed God, keeping, perhaps, such parts of the Torah as they could manage, but holding back from the irrevocable step of circumcision. Now that they knew Jesus Messiah, might this be the time to take on the whole yoke of God?

The opening of the Epistle to the Galatians, the source that reveals that some Gentile believers found the argument for Torah and circumcision attractive, also reveals Paul's reaction to it. It is not just disagreement—it is white-hot indignation. His emotions are so strong as to strain his syntax, and his language becomes so robust that some

English versions translate rather coyly. Paul will not allow it even as an option for people brought up as Hellenistic pagans to adopt, on coming to Christ, the lifestyle of very good, devout, observant Jewish believers. *The followers of Jesus are not proselytes. They are converts.*

This was no unilateral decision of Paul's, though it is he who builds on it a whole understanding of Christian justification, first in Galatians and later in Romans. We are assured in Acts 15 that it reflected the mature decision of the apostles and elders at Jerusalem, and the specific advice of James and of Peter. It marked the church's first critical departure from Jewish tradition and experience. It built cultural diversity into the church forever. What is more, it gave rise to situations that were open-ended and unpredictable.

The Significance of the Convert Model

One way of assessing the significance of the decision of the Jerusalem council that Gentile converts did not, like proselytes, need Torah and circumcision is to consider what the implications of the opposite decision would have been; that is, if the council had decided to retain the long-standing proselyte model and require the new believers to live under the same regime as the original believers in Jesus. It is safe to say that huge areas of Hellenistic social, family, and intellectual life would have been left untouched by Christian faith. Whole stretches of Paul's letters would have been unnecessary. Consider, for instance, the passage in which Paul discusses what a Christian should do if invited to dinner by a pagan friend who may have bought the meat from a temple where it had been offered in pagan sacrifice (1 Cor. 10:27–30). This was an entirely new problem for believers. No apostle or elder, however experienced, had had to face it, because they were all observant Jews, and everyone knew that observant Jews did not sit at pagan dinner tables. Had Corinthian believers become proselytes and adopted the Jerusalem church lifestyle, there would have been no problem; the invitation would not be extended, or would be refused if it were. But Paul envisages a new sort of Christian lifestyle, where believers do join pagans at the dinner table and have to face the implications of acting, thinking, and speaking as Christians in that situation, speaking of Christ, perhaps at a pagan friend's table. He envisages Hellenistic Christians operating within Hellenistic social and family life, challenging and disturbing it, bringing about radical change in it—but from the inside, as a result of Christians expressing the implications of their faith within that society's institutions. Yes, he says in effect, go to dinner with your pagan friend if you want to, but be clear in your mind, and be ready to make clear to people present, the Christian grounds on which you are eating or not taking the meat.

This advice is part of a whole discourse on how Christians should act within the institutions of Hellenistic society (1 Cor. 8:1–11:1). It shows a whole new Jesus lifestyle, a Hellenistic way of being Christian, in process of construction, and we can view much of Paul's correspondence as being essentially about the principles involved in that process. This was necessary because the council of Acts 15 had made it clear that the new believers were not Jewish proselytes, but Greek converts. It was their calling to open up the ways of thinking, speaking, and acting characteristic of Hellenistic society in the Roman East Mediterranean to the influence of Christ. Those ways needed to be turned to him—converted, in fact—until he was enfleshed there, as securely at home in the Hellenistic East Mediterranean as he had been in Jewish Palestine. Paul speaks of himself as being in the pains of childbirth until Christ is formed among the Galatian believers (Gal. 4:19). And Christ could not be formed among them all the time they insisted on patterning themselves on Jewish believers, even exemplary Jewish believers. A Galatian Christ must be formed among Galatian Christians if Galatia was to meet the Christ of God. Is it significant that Paul's tone is harsher with the Galatians, who were, with excellent motives, rejecting the call to a converted Hellenistic lifestyle, than it is with the Corinthians, who were making a mess of constructing one?

In that converted lifestyle every aspect of Hellenistic life and all its institutions must be turned toward Christ. And there were no precedents; the guideposts familiar to early believers were there no longer. At the Jerusalem council no one could have been certain what the converted Hellenistic lifestyle, without the framework of the Torah, would be like—except that it must recall the Christ who walked in Palestine and reflect the activity of the Holy Spirit. Christ would be made flesh once more, made manifest where he had not walked in flesh before, as he was received by faith in Hellenistic society.

Hellenistic social and family life created new situations for believers in Jesus and required Christian choices to be made on a daily basis. The choices were of a different order from those facing dispersion Jews in their cultural adjustment to the Hellenistic world, even though Jews and Christians had so many attitudes in common. Greek-speaking Jews were negotiating someone else's culture while retaining their identity; Greek Christians were negotiating their own culture while expressing a Christian identity. Not only were new social situations constantly arising; an intellectual environment that combined the influences of Greek philosophy, Roman law, Eastern mysticism and spirituality, and astral science was giving rise to questions that no believers had found it necessary to ask before. That intellectual environment was the highway to a great outworking of creative theological activity, but it must have often seemed to old-style Jewish believers to be dangerous, uncharted territory. Had the Jesus community retained the proselyte model, Christians would almost inevitably have been taken out of the intellectual mainstream and shut up to their own sacred books. But as converts, believers in Jesus were required to turn their processes of thought toward Christ, to think Christ into the intellectual framework of their time and place. The eventual result was Christian theology as we know it.

The outcome of conversion was thus culturally and intellectually dynamic, creative, and innovative. As segments of Hellenistic social reality and structures of Hellenistic thought were turned toward Christ, they received new life and meaning. The general effect of the proselyte lifestyle would almost certainly have been to draw the new believers' energies in another direction. It might have produced very devout Christians, but their effect on their society and its ways of thinking would have been negligible.

On many occasions since Galatians was written, good Christian people have tried to ensure that those they have brought to faith would become as much like themselves as possible; have the same priorities and avoidances, hold the same things important, take the Torah and circumcision of those who evangelized them. And it *is* safer. If any conservative-minded Jerusalem believers read 1 Corinthians, they would no doubt have found all their fears about the decision of the Apostolic Council confirmed and would be doubly sure of the folly of leaving raw believers, newly brought out of paganism, without the guidance of the Torah. The way of proselytes is safe. They give up their old customs and beliefs and take up those of someone else. There is a sacrifice involved—they give up their national heritage and social affiliations. But once this is done, the guideposts are clear; there is a precedent for every eventuality; every situation has been met before.

Converts face a much riskier life. Converts have to be constantly, relentlessly turning their ways of thinking, their education and training, their ways of working and doing things, toward Christ. They must think Christ into the patterns of thought they have inherited, into their networks of relationship and their processes for making decisions. And new issues, cultural or intellectual, where it is necessary to make a Christian choice, are arising all the time and with no exact parallels in the past. Proselytes may walk by sight; converts have to walk by faith.

The distinction between proselyte and convert is vital to Christian mission. It springs out of the very origins of that mission, demonstrated in the first great crisis of the early church. The later church has seen many heresies come and go, but the earliest of them has been by far the most persistent. The essence of the "Judaizing" tendency is the insistence on imposing our own religious culture, our own Torah and circumcision. Christian conversion as demonstrated in the New Testament is not about substituting something new for something old—that is to move back to the proselyte model, which the apostolic church could have adopted but decided to abandon. Perhaps they remembered the word of the Lord—his only recorded utterance on the subject of proselytes—that proselytes, won by infinite pains, readily become children of hell (Matt. 23:15). Nor is conversion a case of adding something new to what is already there, a new set of beliefs and values to supplement and refine those already in place. Conversion requires something much more radical. It is less about content than about *direction*. It involves turning the whole personality with its social, cultural, and religious inheritance toward Christ, opening it up to him. It is about turning *what is already there.*

Christ is formed among the elements of the preconversion life as he is received by faith there. And as the Gospel crosses cultural frontiers, many things, as the apostles and elders at Jerusalem realized, are open-ended and unpredictable. The realization would be unbearable but for one thing: the knowledge that new believers receive the Holy Spirit. In the Acts 15 account, it was the fact that God, who knows the heart, had given the Holy Spirit to the Gentiles as well as to the apostolic company; that reality clinched the matter for Peter (Acts 15:8). The Hellenistic way of Christian living would be constructed under the guidance of the Holy Spirit. In a very profound sense conversion is the work of the Holy Spirit in the church.

2

Beyond Bosch: The Early Church and the Christendom Shift

Alan Kreider

David Bosch's *Transforming Mission* is a great book.[1] Its scope is comprehensive; it is, as Lesslie Newbigin put it, a *summa missiologica*. It is in three parts. Part 1, which reflects Bosch's deeply committed study of the New Testament, develops his first paradigm: "the apocalyptic paradigm of primitive Christianity." Part 3, which deals with the contemporary world, explores his sixth paradigm: "an emerging ecumenical missionary paradigm."[2]

Between Bosch's parts 1 and 3, between the New Testament and the contemporary world, lies part 2, "Historical Paradigms of Mission," which I consider in this article. In his part 2 Bosch proposes four epochs in the history of mission, each of which has its own characteristic "paradigm": the missionary paradigm of the Eastern church, which he calls "the Greek patristic period" (p. 190); the medieval Roman Catholic missionary paradigm; the Protestant (Reformation) paradigm; and the modern Enlightenment paradigm.

Bosch acknowledges Hans Küng as originator of this sequence of paradigms. He also recognizes that there are other ways of subdividing the history of the church (p. 188). He refers appreciatively to James P. Martin, who in 1987 proposed a three-epoch periodization: "precritical" ("vitalist," including Küng's Eastern, Roman, and Reformation paradigms), "critical" or "mechanical" (the Enlightenment), and "postcritical" (holistic and ecumenical).[3]

Here I evaluate Bosch's treatment of the early church, which he deals with in his second and third historical paradigms. Having assessed Bosch's chapters on the early church, I propose to join James Martin in suggesting a different, three-paradigm approach to the history of mission.

13

Bosch's Second and Third Paradigms

David Bosch's paradigm 2, "the Greek Patristic period," extends from the late first to the sixth century. In it, Bosch observes, the Christians in the Roman Empire had begun to accommodate themselves to life in the world. They were an illegal religion (*religio illicita*) and hence were liable to periodic bouts of persecution. But their conduct was exemplary, as a result of which they continued to grow, even without the apparent active involvement of missionaries. Bosch's main interest is theological. He traces the developing theology of the Eastern church as it distanced itself from the vivid apocalyptic expectations of primitive Christianity and as it charted its course through the Hellenistic religious environment. Bosch honors the decisions that the theologians of late antiquity made and salutes them for developing theology as a rigorous intellectual discipline. Mission, according to the Eastern Orthodox traditions, emanates from the life of the church as a "sign, symbol and sacrament of the divine" (p. 212). The heartbeat of mission, its very core, is worship—specifically, the Orthodox liturgy. On this point Bosch quotes the twentieth-century theologian Karl Rose: "The light of mercy that shines in the liturgy should act as [the] center of attraction to those who still live in the darkness of paganism" (p. 207). Bosch states what he finds to be limitations in the Orthodox traditions—uncritical inculturation, nationalism, and abandonment of the eschatological urgency of primitive Christianity. But ultimately, Bosch expresses deep respect for the Eastern missionary paradigm, finding at its heart God's love incarnate; for him, John 3:16 is its quintessential missional text.

Paradigm 3, in Bosch's scheme, is "the medieval Roman Catholic missionary paradigm." For Bosch the Middle Ages extends from approximately 600 to 1500. But Bosch finds the roots of the Roman paradigm beginning earlier, with Augustine of Hippo (d. 430) (p. 215). Augustine led the Western church theologically as it shifted the focus from Christ's incarnation to his cross and began to emphasize predestination and original sin. The alliance of the church with the Roman state, begun under Emperor Constantine I early in the fourth century, offered new possibilities for the church in its mission. Augustine was concerned for the spiritual formation of new Christians, but he accorded highest urgency to baptism, which incorporated them sacramentally into the church, within which alone there was salvation. For some years Augustine resisted the idea of compelling pagans or heretics to right belief, but through hard experience he overcame these hesitations (Ep. 93). Augustine thus provided precedents, and a theology, that led to a Western missionary paradigm in which Christians for the first time justified warfare, declared crusades, and launched "waves of forced conversions" across central and northern Europe (p. 226). Nevertheless, Bosch argues, there was throughout the Catholic Middle Ages another missionary model—that of the monks, who by their arduous labors and exemplary life did much to spread the Christian message. And there were some monks, especially in the Celtic traditions, whose commitment to itinerant mission led to remarkable exploits. Bosch is critical in his assessment of the medieval Roman Catholic tradition, as is evident in his choosing Luke 14:23 ("Compel them to come in") as the paradigm's characteristic biblical text. But he is charitable in his assessment of the decisions that the Roman Catholic Christians made. In thinking about the conversion of the emperor Constantine, he joins Lesslie Newbigin in asking, "Could any other choice have been made?" And he judges that the decisions that emanated from this event were logical and inevitable (p. 237). Furthermore, he notes that Roman Catholics since Vatican II have been willing to change. As evidence of this point, we should note that the publisher of *Transforming Mission* is Orbis Books, a distinguished Roman Catholic press.

Bosch, in these historical chapters, proceeds with an unruffled authority. His survey demonstrates both theological acumen and Christian charity. The breadth of his survey does not allow him to make specialist assessments of the various periods, but he has incorporated the work of recognized authorities. I find these chapters attractive, and there is much in them that I agree with.

Difficulties with Bosch's Paradigms

I have three difficulties, however, with Bosch's treatment of the early church in these two paradigms.

Difficulty 1. *It is misleading to speak about the church of the period A.D. 100–600 as "the Eastern [or Greek] Church."* Bosch does so repeatedly. He refers to "the Greek Patristic period" (p. 190) and to "the Greek theology of the early centuries" (p. 210). Bosch shows discomfort with this characterization (p. 203), but it gives a certain ecumenical shape to his project: the early centuries are Orthodox; the medieval are Catholic; the early modern period is Protestant. This is tidy. But I am not happy with it, for two reasons.

First, it is inaccurate. The Christianity of the early centuries was indeed a phenomenon in the Hellenistic world, and the liturgical language, even of Christians in Rome up to the middle of the fourth century, was mainly Greek. But there were growing communities of Christians in the empire whose primary language was Latin. Bosch cites the leader of one of these communities, Cyprian of Carthage, in his treatment of the Eastern church (p. 201); this wording would have astonished Cyprian! Tertullian, the greatest Latin-speaking theologian before Augustine, lived and wrote a half century before Cyprian. The striking thing about the Christianity of this period was how itinerant it was; in Gaul Greek-speaking Christians who had been born in Asia Minor mingled with local Gaulois whose mother tongue was Latin. Christians were amazingly conscious, not of being Eastern or Western, but of being simply Christian—"resident aliens." This sense of commonality extended well beyond the reign of Constantine. In the course of the centuries great controversies about doctrine and jurisdiction arose, which later split the church into Eastern and Western bodies whose languages were Greek and Latin. But this division had not happened by the centuries that Bosch is dealing with in his treatment of the early church.

Second, I find it unfair to label the early centuries "Eastern" and the medieval period "Roman Catholic." By this labeling Bosch ascribes irenic, incarnational qualities to the Eastern church, typified by John 3:16, whereas he attributes compulsion to the Roman church. But across the centuries the Greek-speaking Eastern Christians were every bit as given to arm-twisting and head-bashing as their Latin-speaking Western brothers. "Compel them to come in" well describes the missionary activities of Greek-speaking John of Ephesus, who bludgeoned 80,000 reluctant inhabitants of Asia Minor into the Christian fold in the 540s.[4] It was the emperor Justinian, Constantinople-based, who in 529 introduced legislation that made Christianity the religion of all the empire's inhabitants and who sealed this decision by making infant baptism compulsory (*Codex Iustinianus* 1.11.10). Compulsion is not a Catholic phenomenon or a Western phenomenon; it is a *Christendom* phenomenon. If we insist upon a six-paradigm survey of Christian mission, we do better to follow Scottish missiologist Andrew Walls in calling this age "Hellenistic-Roman."[5]

Difficulty 2. *Bosch's treatment of the early centuries of the church is not that of a historian who draws from the sources; it is that of a theologian who reads other theologians and applies their thinking to earlier times.* A sample of Bosch's theological preoccupation is his treatment of the missionary paradigm of the Eastern church, in which he devotes five pages—one-fifth of the chapter—to contemporary Orthodox theologians. On these pages he does not mention a single ancient Christian writer. These pages can inform us about Orthodox contributions to ecumenical theology of mission today, but they can mislead us about the missionary genius of early Christianity. Let me give two examples.[6]

First, liturgy as a means of mission. Bosch, reading twentieth-century Orthodox writers, appreciates the importance that these writers place upon the liturgy as a tool in evangelization. "Nonbelievers are invited to attend and observe" in these services, which the Orthodox tradition regards as "the main form of witness and mission" (p. 195, also 207–8). This comment no doubt represents late twentieth-century situations in which people from other Christian traditions are attracted to Orthodoxy; it does not, however, reflect the pre-Christendom church. Many years ago liturgical theologian Dom Gregory Dix observed: "The apostolic and primitive church regarded all Christian worship, and especially the eucharist, as a highly *private* activity, and rigidly excluded all strangers from taking any part in it whatsoever, and even from attendance at the eucharist. Christian worship was intensely corporate, but it was not public. . . . It was a highly *exclusive* thing, whose original setting is entirely domestic and private."[7]

The sources are clear on this point: only the baptized and those being prepared for baptism (the catechumens) could be admitted to the first part of the Lord's Day services—the service of the Word (readings and sermon); and only the baptized could be admitted to the second part, or the service of the Eucharist (prayers and communion). A deacon was stationed at the door of the church to keep the outsiders out![8] This approach seems counterintuitive: how does a church grow rapidly if it excludes inquirers until they have gone through a rigorous regimen of catechesis and initiation? In my writing I have struggled with this question and have concluded that worship—the liturgy—was indeed central to the growth of the early church, but for reasons very different from that stated by Bosch. The liturgy was central because it edified and formed Christians and Christian communities who were free in Christ and fascinating to outsiders.[9] To be sure, in the early years of Christendom, worship services came to be missionary in intent: Christian leaders hoped that the sheer splendor of the gold and jewels in the buildings, the rhetorical eloquence of the sermons, and the magnificence of the ritual would move the nonbaptized to request baptism. The leaders facilitated this approach by lowering the hurdles to becoming a catechumen (e.g., children were often made catechumens at birth).[10] But soon this approach was no longer necessary. In Christendom, from the sixth century onward, infant baptism was normal practice, and everyone was by law Christian, so the missionary quality of the liturgy no longer mattered.

Second, the centrality of doctrine. Bosch (p. 195) correctly observes the preeminent value that the Eastern church gave to "definitive statements of faith." In the New Testament, he notes, there was an emphasis upon God's participation in saving events in history, which "the Greeks" superseded by emphasizing correct statements about God. Bosch illustrates this shift of focus by contrasting the Sermon on the Mount with the Nicene Creed; the former is concerned with conduct, the latter, with metaphysics. This contrast is indeed striking. But Bosch does not address the questions of *how* and *when* the church moved from ethics to dogmatics. Was the church of the early centuries as preoccupied with ontology as the theologians of Nicaea? Was the Sermon on the Mount a peripheral concern in the missionary activity of the pre-Nicene church?

Bosch does not help us here, but the early church sources can. Justin, a teacher from Palestine who was martyred in Rome in 165, in his First *Apology* summarized the teachings of the Sermon on the Mount, and then commented (p. 16): "Those who are found not living as he [Christ] taught should know that they are not really Christians, even if his teachings are on their lips." Athenagoras, writing a quarter of a century later in Athens, responded to a frequent question: "What are the teachings on which we are brought up? 'I say to you, love them who curse you, pray for them who persecute you, that you may be the sons of your Father in heaven.' . . . In our ranks . . . you could find common men, artisans, and old women who, if they cannot establish by reasoned discourse the usefulness of their teaching, show by deed the usefulness of the exercise of their will. For they do not rehearse words but show forth good deeds; when struck, they do not strike back" (*Legatio* 11). The earlier church, Greek as well as Roman, emphasized the missionary attractiveness of transformed lives, and Jesus' teaching indicated what these transformed lives should look like. Nowhere does a pre-Christendom writer say that the Sermon on the Mount is unimportant, or that ordinary Christians cannot live its teachings.[11] In pre-Christendom, non-Christians were not attracted by glorious liturgy or by superbly crafted theology; rather, they were drawn to faith in Christ by means of Christians and Christian communities who, because Jesus' teachings were a living reality in their midst, were free, intriguing, attractive.

Difficulty 3. *Bosch's paradigms are theological (his subtitle is* Paradigm Shifts in Theology of Mission*) but not practical; he thus overlooks the fundamental paradigm shift in Christianity's first millennium—the Christendom* *shift*.[12] Historically, midway through Bosch's "Missionary Paradigm of the Eastern Church," something astonishing happened—the Roman emperor Constantine declared that he was a Christian. It took several centuries before the changes resulting from this event became solidified. But they were far-reaching indeed, leading to the advent of the Christian civilization that in the West has been called Christendom. Nothing, I believe, changed missionary practice and theology more than this development. Bosch is of course aware of the impact of Constantine's conversion; he notes that after the Edict of Milan, which in 313 granted Christianity legal status alongside other religions in the empire, "the situation was to change dramatically" (p. 202). This edict led to a compromise between the church and the emperor whereby "the emperor was to rule in 'time' and Christ in 'eternity.'" Bosch obviously regretted this development (p. 222).

But I do not think that Bosch came to terms with the advent of Christendom and its consequences for mission. He mentions Christendom briefly (pp. 274–75), and as we have just noted, he saw that Constantine's reign changed the situation "dramatically." But from his perspective, it was not a change dramatic enough to constitute a paradigm shift in mission. I beg to disagree. Bosch's title indicates that his concern is with *Transforming Mission*. I believe that there is nothing more transforming of mission—missional thought and missional praxis—than the coming of Christendom in both West and East. Christendom sought to subject all areas of human experience to the lordship of Christ.[13] In this aim it had varied success, but it entailed things that I find troubling missionally: a marriage between Christianity and state power, between Christianity and compulsion, and between Christianity and conventional values. Below, I discuss the missional implications of the coming of Christendom under eight categories.

First, however, a word about Constantine himself. In 312, early in his career, on the eve of a decisive battle, Constantine had a vision—he saw a cross of light, with the inscription "Conquer by This." The emperor, deeply moved, ordered a cross to be constructed. "A spear, overlaid with gold," was made into a cross by attaching a transverse bar, on top of which was a wreath of gold and precious stones containing the Chi-Rho, or Christogram; hanging from the crossbar was an embroidered cloth laden with precious stones. The emperor henceforth used this cross as a "safeguard in all engagements with his enemies" (Eusebius, *Vita Constantini* [*VC*] 1.29, 31). What progress for the cross! From an instrument of the empire's scornful violence that killed a provincial Jew accused of being a revolutionary, to a gesture by powerless Christians to invoke spiritual power for divine protection in danger ("sign of the passion," *Apostolic Tradition* [attrib. to Hippolytus] 42a), to a gold-bedecked statement of the emperor's adherence to Christianity—the cross has come a long way. After his dream, Constantine did not immediately become a Christian,[14] although he did take steps to benefit Christianity. Not only did he end persecution, but he showered privileges upon Christian clergy, made Sunday a legal holiday for all, presided at the ecumenical council at Nicaea (325), and built elaborate church buildings, one of which he decorated with "purest gold" so that its interior would "glitter as it were with rays of light" (*VC* 3.36).[15] Furthermore, he admitted bishops to his table, even though they were "mean in their attire and outward appearance" (*VC* 1.42).

Christianity had found a home—at court. Here was as graphic an expression as one could imagine of the transforming of mission. Here, in stark relief, was evidence of a massive paradigm shift. Not everything changed overnight in the church's approach to mission; it took a century or more for the effects of this transformation to be worked out. In the 360s, in Asia Minor, Basil of Caesarea was still attempting to train his baptismal candidates so they would be "conformed to the teaching of our Lord Jesus Christ like wax to the mould" (*On Baptism* 1.2.10). But in this respect Basil was conservative, maintaining traditional emphases in a world that was changing. For a corner was being turned, a paradigm was shifting. I find it helpful to think of this shift—the "Christendom shift"—using language of inculturation (which Bosch discusses beginning on p. 447). Bosch refers his readers to Andrew Walls, who proposes two principles necessary for the insertion of Christianity in any culture: the *indigenizing principle*, which calls for the Gospel to express itself in forms and language native to a society, and the *pilgrim principle*, by which the Gospel expresses universal values that challenge any society.[16] Christians have always struggled to balance these two principles. In pre-Christendom the Christians may have tended, by external pressure or habit, to overstress the pilgrim principle; in Christendom Christians may have been too confident in their indigenizing, thereby losing the sense of being distinctive.

Shifting from Pre-Christendom to Christendom

Let us consider and contrast these two critical missionary paradigms— "pre-Christendom" and "Christendom"—in terms of eight categories, as shown in the accompanying table.

1. Vantage point. *The Christendom shift moved the perspective of Christians from the margins of society to its center.* In pre-Christendom, before Constantine, Christianity was a *religio illicita*, an illegal superstition that could result in harassment by neighbors or persecution by the imperial authorities. Christianity was socially inclusive (women as well as men, educated and uneducated, poor and wealthy), but those at the apex of society—aristocratic males—were rarely attracted to it. When aristocrats came to faith, some of them, such as Cyprian, had to give up wealth and power to become free as Christians (*Ad Donatum* 3).[17] Christians were excluded from centers of power, so they developed decentralized forms of life; their communities met in domestic settings (*domus ecclesiae*). They

The Christendom Paradigm Shift: Mission

Category	Pre-Christendom	Christendom
Vantage point	margins; deviant; private	center; mainstream; public
Attraction	free humans; attractive community; spiritual power	access to prestige/jobs/power; participation in society
Power	spiritual power; human vulnerability	human/institutional power
Sanctions	voluntary	compulsory
Inculturation	pilgrim and indigenizing principles in tension; resident aliens	indigenizing principle predominates; residents
Role of Jesus	The Good Shepherd—Victor, Lord, healer, teacher for all Christians	*Pantokrator*—exalted as God, teacher for "perfect" Christians
Worship	unimpressive; equipping Christians to live attractive lives	dramatic liturgy in imposing buildings; impressing non-Christians
Missional style	mission as the identity of the church; taking the pagan and Jewish options seriously	maintenance as the stance of the church; proscribing the pagan and Jewish options; mission to backsliding believers or to people on the frontiers

saw the world, read the Bible, and did theology, not from the top or the center, but from the margins. In pre-Christendom, a convert went "from ordinary citizen to fanatical member of a group that . . . deviates from the norms of the wider society."[18]

In Christendom, Christians came to occupy central positions in society. Constantine's sharing his table with the bishops showed this upward movement happening. Christians were no longer deviant. Indeed, Christianity had become the religion of the imperial establishment. Converting to Christianity now meant being "won over to the norms that society at large upholds."[19] So the aristocratic males began to join the church, whose values and traditions they proceeded to alter to conform to the values that their class had long espoused. The imperial governor Ambrose, unlike Cyprian, did not change fundamentally upon his baptism; instead, he proceeded to write a Christian equivalent of the "Duties" (*De officiis*) of Cicero, to indicate how Christian clergy and literate laity should behave.[20] An "aristocratization" of the Christian world ensued.[21] Acts of worship were now public, taking place in basilicas rather than houses.[22] Christians now saw the world and interpreted the Bible and did theology, not from the margins, but from the center.

2. Attraction. *The Christendom shift buttressed Christianity's appeal with imposing incentives, thereby changing the nature of its attraction.* In pre-Christendom, non-Christians were attracted by the countercultural freedom, justice, and joy of the Christians. People who were attracted to Christianity faced imposing disincentives. Some of these were imposed by the wider society. Christians encountered harassment and ostracism from their non-Christian neighbors; at times they even faced execution. The Christian church also imposed its own disincentives to cheap conversion; its lengthy catechetical program helped ensure that converts were genuine.[23] Nevertheless, despite these deterrents, people persisted in becoming Christian at an astonishing rate.[24] Why did they join? Time and again, the testimony was the same—people were attracted to Christianity because Christians were attractive. Origen stated, "The churches of God which have been taught by Christ, when compared with the assemblies of the people where they live, are 'as lights in the world'" (*Contra Celsum* 3.29). Justin reported that people's hesitations were overcome "by observing the consistent lives of their neighbors, or noting the strange patience of their injured acquaintances, or experiencing the way they did business with them" (Justin, *1 Apol.* 16). Christian leaders thus attempted to equip the Christians to be attractively distinctive. Their catechesis aimed to form Christians whose lives "may shine with virtue, not before each other [only], but also before the Gentiles so they may imitate them and become Christians" (*Canons of Hippolytus* 19). Their sermons sought to keep the believers to their commitments to attractive deviance (see *2 Clement* 13). As one pre-Christendom apologist summed it up, "We [Christians] do not preach great things, but we live them" (Minucius Felix, *Octavius* 38.6).

In Christendom the disincentives to conversion were replaced by incentives. People became Christians for many reasons, but not least because it was the emperor's religion. Christianity now provided access to professional advancement. It did not take long before people were complaining, in a way they never did in pre-Christendom, of "the scandalous hypocrisy of those who crept into the church, and assumed the name and character of Christians" (*VC* 4.54). People of social eminence and economic power became Christian and then told their underlings that it would be to their advantage to convert. Augustine characterized a typical candidate for baptism in early fifth-century Hippo as a socially inferior person who seeks "to derive some benefit from men whom he thinks he could not otherwise please, or to escape some injury at the hands of men whose displeasure or enmity he dreads" (*First Baptismal Instruction* 5.9). In Christendom, people at times still became Christian because of the believers' attractive qualities, but the biggest disincentive to conversion was now often the Christians themselves. As Augustine noted in one of his sermons (15.6), "When someone is pressing him [a pagan] to believe, he will answer, 'Do you want me to be like that so-and-so and the other?'" Non-Christians now resisted conversion on moral grounds. The ultimate answer of the Christendom church was force.

3. Power. *The Christendom shift moved the church's reliance from divine to human power.* In pre-Christendom the Christians had very little power. Gradually, as time passed, the movement came to have some friends, especially women, at the imperial court. And the attractiveness of Christians and their communities led some locally prominent citizens (*decurions*) to join the church. But even these knew that they, in a crisis, might lose their lives. Perhaps because they had little political power, pre-Christendom Christians are recorded as relying upon God's power.[25] Tertullian noted that people were drawn to Christianity because of the *magnalia* (miraculous happenings) that occurred in their meetings (*To His Wife* 2.7). Origen reported that people came to faith "in spite of themselves, some spirit having turned their mind suddenly from hating the Gospel to dying for it by means of a vision by day or night" (*Contra Celsum* 1.46). Exorcisms were at the heart of the catechetical procedures by which Christians prepared candidates for baptism.[26] Everett Ferguson has concluded that "an important factor in the Christian success in the Roman world was the promise which it made of deliverance from demons."[27]

After the Christendom shift the exorcisms continued, and in preparations for baptism they became ever more dramatic and terrifying.[28] Miracles were reported in association with relics of saints and also on the edges of Christendom, in the East and the West, where "holy men" lived and where missionaries encountered opposition. But in Christendom's heartlands, where Christians had power, miracles soon became a thing of the past. As Ambrose commented in Milan, "In the beginning there were signs for the sake of unbelievers; but for us who live in the time of the church's full growth, the truth is to be grasped, not by signs, but by faith" (*De sacramentis* 2.15). God's power was now experienced in more predictable, institutional ways.

4. Sanctions. *The Christendom shift changed Christianity from a voluntary movement to a compulsory institution.* In pre-Christendom believers came to faith and baptism despite formidable disincentives. In a world where fate, demons, and social conventions kept people in bondage, they saw their conversion as an assertion of freedom. As Justin observed, "At our first birth we were born of necessity without our knowledge," but in baptism the Christians had been reborn through their "free choice and knowledge" (*1 Apol.* 61). Cyprian gave as one of the fundamental principles of the North African church that "the liberty of believing or not believing is placed in free choice" (*Ad Quirinum* 3.52). Christianity was therefore incompatible with force or compulsion, for the God whom the Christians worshiped did not work "by violent means . . . but by means of persuasion" (Irenaeus, *Adv. Haer.* 5.1.1). The Christian church was growing rapidly, but it was growing freely, voluntarily, as an invitation to a rich and adventurous life, from the bottom up.

In the fourth century this situation gradually changed. Basil of Caesarea, writing in Cappadocia in the 360s, was deeply committed to a pre-Christendom approach: "One must not use human advantages in preaching the Gospel, lest the grace of God be obscured thereby" (*Moralia* 70.26). But by the last decades of the century, powerful Christians regarded this view as old fashioned and found ways to make Christianity compulsory. These ways, according to Ramsay MacMullen, were typically "laws, monks, and landowners."[29] Laws passed in 380 and 392 deprived "heretical" Christians and pagans of the freedom to worship in public (*Codex Theodosianus* 16.10.2; 16.1.2). As Augustine noted approvingly, "For long Christians did not dare answer a pagan; now, thank God, it is a crime to remain a pagan" (*Enarr. in Ps.* 88). Churchmen worked together with provincial governors to despoil pagan temples and shrines. The role of the monks is less familiar. Bosch noted the contribution of monks in spreading the Gospel throughout Europe, sometimes by their active preaching and often by the "missionary dimension" of their common life (p. 233). At their best the monks were also committed to spiritual disciplines of repentance, reconciliation, and hospitality, "taking on the nonviolent identity of Jesus."[30] But the monks also, especially in the East, provided shock troops for de-paganization.[31] The role of landowners in converting their peasants is unsurprising. When landowners were motivated to do so, they could require peasants to present themselves for baptism—or else. "If such a proprietor became a Christian," Augustine commented, "no one would remain a pagan" (*Enarr. in Ps.* 54.13). A final way of making Christianity compulsory, which MacMullen did not mention and which Bosch ignored, was infant baptism. In pre-Christendom this practice had been exceptional, even in Christian homes, but in the fifth century a "baptismal revolution" made it the norm, and the infants had no choice.[32] In Christendom the sanctions had shifted. Instead of non-Christians overcoming disincentives to become Christian, now non-Christians had to overcome tremendous pressure if they wished to continue to be pagan or Jewish. In the Christianized countries of Europe, few of them did so. Christianity, which had been a voluntary assertion of freedom, had become a compulsory inevitability. The church, in Christendom, grew from the top down.

5. Inculturation. *The Christendom shift caused Christianity to be at home in society, so that it lost the capacity to make a distinctive contribution to society.* In pre-Christendom, especially in the first and second centuries, the word that Christians habitually used to describe themselves was "resident aliens" (*paroikoi*). Christians were conscious of being at home, but also not fully at home, wherever they lived: "Every foreign country is a fatherland to them, and every fatherland is foreign" (*Ep. Diognetus* 5). To maintain this sense of distinctiveness in the midst of a larger society, the churches developed careful prebaptismal catecheses. This training, which could last for several years, imparted to the apprentice Christians the narratives of the Bible, the teachings of Jesus, and the ethics and folkways of the Christian community. An experienced Christian who served as sponsor (or godparent) accompanied the baptismal candidate at these teaching sessions.[33] By these means, new Christians were equipped to join a church that was attempting to inculturate the faith with fidelity—being at home in society (the indigenizing principle) while remaining true to Christianity's distinctive convictions (the pilgrim principle). Christians constantly weighed which practices and symbols of the wider society they could appropriate and Christianize, and which they must repudiate. Some of their decisions were fascinating. For example, many Christians adopted the *refrigerium*, the funerary meal, to celebrate the anniversaries of the death of the Christians, despite its associations with paganism and overindulgence.[34]

In Christendom, as the church grew even more rapidly and began to infiltrate the imperial elite, indigenizing tendencies were heightened, and the pilgrim principle came under strain. Roman aristocrats were understandably uncomfortable with the centuries-old customs and traditions of Christianity. Augustine, late in the fourth century, met this uneasiness in Volusian, a Roman administrator in North Africa who was cautiously exploring Christianity. Volusian informed Augustine that "the preaching and doctrine [of Christ] were not adaptable to the customs of the state." Augustine corrected his correspondent. The teachings of Jesus that alarmed Volusian referred only to "the interior dispositions of the heart," not to political behavior, which could be guided by "a sort of kindly harshness." A Roman aristocrat could safely become a Christian without having to challenge the values of his class (Augustine, *Epp.* 136–37). Augustine's exchange with Volusian illustrates the process of "aristocratization" that was taking place throughout the Christian church in the century after Constantine. On point after point, Christian leaders smoothed off the angularities of the Christian tradition so that Christianity could fit neatly into a society that would be dominated by its traditional elite who were now presenting themselves for baptism. Fourth-century teaching for baptismal candidates concentrated, not on how to live the teachings of Jesus, but on how to avoid the errors of heresy.[35] Literature began to appear to guide the behavior of the Christianized aristocrats. In the 380s Bishop Ambrose of Milan wrote *De officiis* (Of the duties), a Christian appropriation of the similarly titled work by the pagan Cicero, to make the church intelligible to the elite and to claim the elite's territory as its own.[36] At this time and in this way the just-war theory entered Christian history. The just-war theory, like Ambrose's *De officiis*, was an exercise in inculturation. It was an expression of Christianity's indigenization into the world of the imperial elite, whose discomfort was allayed by a softening and interiorizing of Jesus' "love your enemies" teaching. Elite values (i.e., traditional Roman values) now dominated public life.[37] And the Christians were ceasing to be pilgrims; in the medieval West, Christians were known, not as resident aliens (Gk. *paroikoi*), but as "residents/parishioners" (Lat. *parochiani*).

6. Role of Jesus. *The Christendom shift transformed the role of Jesus in the church from the Good Shepherd, who was teacher of all Christians, to the exalted Lord, whose teaching was applicable to a minority of "perfect" Christians.* In pre-Christendom, Christian iconography depicted Jesus as the Good Shepherd, healer, and teacher. This imagery accorded with a central theme in early Christianity—the life-giving power of Jesus' teaching. In North Africa around 250, Bishop Cyprian called Jesus "the Lord, the teacher of our life and master of eternal salvation," who provided "divine commands" and "precepts of heaven" that were to guide all believers (*On Works and Alms* 7).

In Christendom, as Bosch rightly observed, Christians "underexposed" Christ's humanness and depicted him "in terms reminiscent of the emperor cult" (p. 202). Jesus the Good Shepherd, healer, and teacher disappeared; in his place came Christ the *Pantokrator* (ruler of all), exalted, dressed as an emperor, with the imperial nimbus around his head.[38] A sample of this "new look" comes from the Church of San Vitale in Ravenna, neatly poised culturally between East and West. Its visual climax, the apse mosaic, depicts Christ, resplendent in gold and jewels; under him, carrying the chalice and paten for the Eucharist, are Emperor Justinian and Empress Theodora.[39] This Christ is not one of us. The Arian controversy had shown the "orthodox" that it was necessary to de-emphasize Christ's humanity and to highlight his divinity so that his teaching could be appropriated, and his example could be imitated, only by special, ascetic Christians.[40] So a new, dual-level, Christian ethic appeared; it had its roots in previous centuries, but in Christendom it came to full flower.[41] Eusebius of Caesarea expressed it concisely in the 330s: "Two ways of living were thus given by the law of Christ to his church. The one is above nature, and beyond common human living; it admits not marriage, childbearing, property, nor possession of wealth, but wholly and permanently separate from the common customary life of mankind, it devotes itself to the service of God alone in its wealth of heavenly love. . . . Such is the perfect form of the Christian life. And the other more humble, more human, permits men to join in pure nuptials and to produce children, to undertake government, to give orders to soldiers fighting for right. . . . [This is] a kind of secondary grade of piety" (*Demonstratio Evangelica* 1.8.29b–30b).

Ambrose, in his *De officiis*, picked up the same theme, not to depreciate his lay readers, but to give them a clear sense of the possible. It was, he argued, only the "perfect" celibates who were to "love our enemies, and pray for those that falsely accuse and persecute us" (1.36–37, 129, 175–77). The exalted Christ could do this; so also, with difficulty, could the clergy who would be perfect. But such behavior was not possible, and not desirable, for the ordinary Christian aristocrat who was to love his neighbor (if not his enemy) by defending cities and administering estates. If Christ was not the role model for the Christians, who then was? According to Ambrose it was the patriarchs. In *De officiis* he pointed to a succession of Old Testament role models—but not to Jesus, who, in a world where everyone was Christian, was a model for religious professionals.

7. Worship. *The Christendom shift transformed worship from humble gatherings that edified Christians to grand assemblies that attempted to evangelize outsiders.* In pre-Christendom churches, worship services were generally small in scale, domestic in setting, rhetorically unpolished, ritually unimpressive, and restricted to Christians. Their aim was not to impress the masses but rather to worship God, equipping the Christians as individuals and communities to live their faith attractively. To this end, worship fed them with spiritual food, from the Word and table, necessary to sustain them as they followed Jesus in a dangerous world.

In Christendom, Christian services still attempted to facilitate worship of God, but their social function changed. They became public, glorious in ornately decorated basilicas. Attendance was at times compulsory, with some people irritated at being forced to be there, others eager to be entertained. People misbehaved; in Syria the deacons circulated in the services to ensure that the people would not "whisper, nor slumber, nor laugh, nor nod" (*Apostolic Constitutions* 2.57). Worship, like the buildings, was designed to move the congregation emotionally, to give them an overwhelming experience of God, who was being revealed to them in the awe-inspiring rituals.[42] In the early years of Christendom the services attempted to attract unbaptized catechumens to submit their names for baptism. As means of evangelizing those present, the services employed gifted rhetorical preachers, grand liturgies, and symbolism and artifacts that were society's highest indicators of value—gold, jewels, and imperial imagery. Johannes Quasten has noted that "more and more the liturgy changed shape from the simple celebration of the Lord's Supper, as it had been celebrated in the houses of the first Christians, to a court ceremonial, to a royal reception."[43]

In pre-Christendom, worship was for Christians, to prepare them to live in evangelical attractiveness; in Christendom, worship was aimed at the half-committed and the uncommitted, to dazzle and convert the reluctant masses.

8. Missional style. *The Christendom shift altered the focus of the church from mission to maintenance, except on the fringes of the "Christian" territories.* In pre-Christendom, mission was central to the identity of the church. The centrality of mission is something about which the early Christians wrote very little. But one can see it in the topics that the Christians dealt with in their writings. A significant proportion of early Christian writings were "apologies," showing that they took their pagan and Jewish neighbors seriously and were working to find ways to converse with them. Another sample of mission at the heart of the identity of the early

Christians is an odd document coming from North Africa in the late 240s. It is a collection of 120 precepts that Cyprian prepared to guide the church in Carthage. He included the following: "that we must labor not with words, but with deeds"; "that the Holy Spirit has frequently appeared in fire"; "that widows and orphans ought to be protected" (*Ad Quirinum* 3.96, 101, 113). Nowhere among the 120 precepts did he admonish the faithful to evangelize. And yet the church was growing rapidly because Christians were living attractively, alert to the concerns of their non-Christian neighbors, and "chattering" unself-consciously to them about their faith. And they were doing these things so naturally that they did not need Cyprian to lecture them to do so.

In Christendom it ceased to be natural to be missionary. The church grew, aided by imperial favor and legislation, until by the sixth century it came to include all inhabitants of the empire. Those who held out against conversion were bludgeoned into conformity. A law of Emperor Justinian of 529 symbolized the end of this process and also indicated the difficulties it had faced. This law observed that some people who had been baptized "have been found possessed by the error of unholy and abominable pagans and doing those things which move the Benevolent God to wrath." Some people were even teaching "the insanity of the unholy pagans" to others, thereby "destroy[ing] the instructed persons' souls." These people were to be subject to "vengeance proper to their convicted sins." Anyone who had not yet been baptized was to approach the churches, "along with their wives and children and all the household belonging to them," to be taught and baptized; their young children were all to be baptized immediately. Anyone who resisted this law was not to be allowed to own property but was to be "abandoned in poverty," besides being subjected to unspecified "appropriate penalties."[44] Here was a new form of mission! No longer did Christians have to take the pagan and Jewish options seriously, for force had won the argument.[45] So Christians could devote their literary talents to defining orthodoxy and to defaming the heterodox. By imperial law, which made everyone an orthodox Christian, mission was unnecessary.

But even in Christendom, mission kept intruding. Pastorally astute people were aware that many people had been lightly Christianized— poorly catechized, scarcely converted. Baptized Christians continued to engage in subterranean pagan practices, which they combined with attendance at Mass. A churchful of people was also certain to contain a large number of "depraved persons" (Augustine, *First Catechetical Instruction* 7.12). So there was always the case for "inner mission" to revive the ardor of the faithless "faithful." And then there was mission on the frontiers of the Christian world. There, where Christians met pagans, missionary encounter could still take place. It might be genuine, or (alas!) it might lead to conversion by conquest.[46]

Reflections on the Christendom Shift

These eight categories, I contend, define a paradigm shift in mission in the fourth century—the Christendom shift. This schematization, like any attempt to bring conceptual clarity to historical change, is too neat. It overlooks anticipations, such as the many signs of growing respectability in the churches of the third century.[47] Also, it ignores the ways in which examples of early radicalism continued to occur a century and a half after Constantine; for example, the Alexandrine Sinodos, a fifth-century Coptic church order, stipulated that a soldier shall be admitted as a catechumen "only if he leaves that [military] occupation."[48] Historical change is always untidy.

Nevertheless, in missiological terms the Christendom shift is important. Of Bosch's six paradigms, three—the Eastern, Roman Catholic, and Reformation (Protestant)—have more in common with each other than they do with pre-Christendom; or four, if one includes the Enlightenment paradigm, whose worldview was profoundly shaped by Christendom. In each of our eight categories of mission, the Eastern, Roman Catholic, Reformation, and Enlightenment paradigms are strikingly similar to one another, and markedly different from the church that preceded Constantine. If I am right here, the most profound paradigm shift occurred in the fourth century. That century, which brought the early church to a conclusion and ushered in Christendom, is truly the century that befits Bosch's title "transforming mission."

Christendom was in many respects admirable. The Holy Spirit continued to be active in the church, and saints and scholars, missionaries and artists from the Christendom centuries have bequeathed a rich legacy to subsequent Christians. Furthermore, there were things that the pre-Christendom church had not worked out. The theological issues that preoccupied (too greatly?) the church of the fourth and fifth centuries were lurking in the third century, and they needed to be addressed.

Nevertheless I, like James P. Martin, propose that we think not of six but of three historical paradigms of mission: *pre-Christendom, Christendom*, and *post-Christendom*. The first two of these I have discussed in some detail. The third, Christians are exploring in many countries in the West as Christendom's institutions and assumptions stagger on or disintegrate.

This threefold succession of paradigms works, in a rough and ready way, for the United States and western Europe. In the United States theologians debate whether America's Christendom era is over; recent developments may indicate that it is experiencing a resurgence.[49] In most countries in Europe the issue is more clear-cut; there theologians have begun to write books about "mission after Christendom" and to develop a distinctive style of church life and evangelization for the post-Christendom era.[50] The pre-Christendom church, they are discovering, can be a resource and conversation partner for them as they find their way through uncharted territory.[51]

In other parts of the world, outside of historic Christendom territories, the threefold distinction of pre-Christendom, Christendom, and post-Christendom paradigms can also be useful. Churches in many countries were founded by Western missionaries who imported Christendom assumptions and institutions as an integral part of the Gospel. Increasingly the leaders of these churches are finding that they must listen anew to their own cultures, and to the pastoral realities that they face, for their churches are suffering from nominalism, and their people are unattractive, demonstrating a lack of Christian integrity at work, and their life and worship are unappealing to young people. People in these churches often find that pre-Christendom is fascinating. For them, pre-Christendom patterns can provide a means of critiquing the Christendom practices and assumptions that are weighing their churches down and can point ways forward toward a hopeful future.

There are other churches throughout history, and also today, for which Christendom has never had relevance. I think of the Church of the East (called "Nestorian" by outsiders), which had remarkable success in evangelizing central and east Asia in the first millennium, and which has demonstrated that a tradition can be simultaneously non-Christendom and liturgical.[52] I think also of the many churches around the world today that have sprung spontaneously to life within the past half century. These churches have not been shaped primarily by the West. The pre-Christendom, Christendom, and post-Christendom paradigms do not apply to them. Indeed, Christendom is of little interest to them—their life experience is close to that of the primitive church.[53] But when they learn about the pre-Christendom church, their interest perks up. They say, "That's just like us!" Or, "That's really useful to us!"[54] Despite this fascination with the early church, these churches may be tempted to make decisions about mission and inculturation that are very similar to those that fourth-century Christians made. For them, a study of the Christendom shift can be prophetic, a source of sobriety and caution.[55]

Whatever the situation—in the West, in the Christendom-affected global church, or in the new churches of the world—I find that the early, pre-Christendom churches speak with freshness and hope. In the last section of his book, David Bosch writes of "the emergence of a postmodern paradigm." Although Bosch does not say so, I believe that this is also implicitly a "post-Christendom" paradigm. Many of Bosch's insights will be useful in equipping Christians for life in this peculiar, fascinating, wonderful era in which Christians are less and less encumbered with power. So also, if we have an ear to hear, will be the insights of the early Christians who lived before the Christendom shift.

Notes

1. David J. Bosch, *Transforming Mission: Paradigm Shifts in Theology of Mission* (Maryknoll, N.Y.: Orbis Books, 1991). An earlier version of this article appeared as "Beyond Bosch: The Early Church and the Christendom Shift," *Mission Focus: Annual Review* 11 (2003): Supplement, pp. 158–77.
2. Cf. Wilbert R. Shenk, "Recasting Theology of Mission: Impulses from the Non-Western World," *International Bulletin of Missionary Research* 25 (July 2001): 98–107.
3. James P. Martin, "Toward a Post-Critical Paradigm," *New Testament Studies* 33 (1987): 370–85.
4. Ramsay MacMullen, *Christianity and Paganism in the Fourth to Eighth Centuries* (New Haven: Yale Univ. Press, 1997), pp. 66–67.
5. Andrew F. Walls, *The Missionary Movement in Christian History: Studies in the Transmission of Faith* (Maryknoll, N.Y.: Orbis Books, 1996), pp. 18–20.
6. A third example has to do with Bosch's treatment of eschatology. On the one hand Bosch sees eschatology as definitional, as a way of differentiating his second paradigm from his first ("the apocalyptic paradigm of primitive Christianity"). I find that Bosch, in the area of eschatology as well as in the other two areas that I cite, introduces later theology into the early centuries. And yet he hedges his bets. On p. 198 he observes that a realistic eschatology including chiliasm, bodily resurrection, and the reign of the saints with Christ "was upheld by those Christians who formed the solid body of the church and contributed the majority of its martyrs," a statement that can be borne out by the sources. I therefore find his second paradigm to be incoherent. If it is to be resuscitated, the area of eschatology needs emergency treatment!
7. Dom Gregory Dix, *The Shape of the Liturgy*, rev. ed. (London: Adam & Charles Black, 1945), pp. 16, 35.
8. *Testamentum Domini* 1.36.
9. Alan Kreider, *Worship and Evangelism in Pre-Christendom* (Cambridge: Grove Books, 1995), pp. 8–9.

10. A prime example would be Augustine of Hippo. See his *Confessions* 1.11.17.

11. Karlmann Beyschlag, "Zur Geschichte der Bergpredigt in der alten Kirche," *Zeitschrift für Theologie und Kirche* 74 (1977): 297.

12. Stuart Murray discusses the Christendom shift in chapter 4 of his book *Post-Christendom* (Carlisle, Eng.: Paternoster Press, 2004).

13. For a description of the characteristics of Christendom, see Alan Kreider, *The Change of Conversion and the Origin of Christendom* (Harrisburg, Pa.: Trinity Press International, 1999), pp. 91–98.

14. Ibid., chap. 4; H. A. Drake, *Constantine and the Bishops: The Politics of Intolerance* (Baltimore: Johns Hopkins Univ. Press, 2000), pp. 419–20.

15. Upon conversion, Constantine decided to "patronize the church using the full panoply of imperial wealth and wealth-based propaganda" (Dominic Janes, *God and Gold in Late Antiquity* [Cambridge: Cambridge Univ. Press, 1998], p. 113).

16. Walls, *Missionary Movement*, pp. 7–9.

17. For a discussion of the downward mobility evident in Cyprian's conversion, see Kreider, *Change of Conversion*, pp. 7–9.

18. Wayne A. Meeks, *The Origins of Christian Morality: The First Two Centuries* (New Haven: Yale Univ. Press, 1993), p. 21.

19. Ibid.

20. Ivor J. Davidson, "Staging the Church? Theology as Theater," *Journal of Early Christian Studies* 8 (2000): 413–51.

21. Michele Renee Salzman, *The Making of a Christian Aristocracy: Social and Religious Change in the Western Roman Empire* (Cambridge, Mass: Harvard Univ. Press, 2002), p. 219.

22. In the fourth and fifth centuries, in keeping with long-established tradition, Christian worship services remained private, that is, open solely to the baptized (the Eucharist) and the catechumens and baptized (the service of the Word). But as a result of the devaluation of the catechumenate and the spread of infant baptism, the majority of the populace now qualified for admission to services. Hence my statement that Christian worship in Christendom had become public.

23. *Apostolic Tradition* 16–20.

24. Rodney Stark, *The Rise of Christianity: A Sociologist Reconsiders History* (Princeton: Princeton Univ. Press, 1996), p. 6. Cf. Bosch in *Transforming Mission*, who says, contrary to all the evidence: "For a while, the church had to forfeit its opportunity for rapid growth; it devoted its time and energy to finding clarity on crucial theological issues and to consolidating internally" (p. 200).

25. James A. Kelhoffer, *Miracle and Mission: The Authentication of Missionaries and Their Message in the Longer Ending of Mark* (Tübingen: Mohr Siebeck, 2000), pp. 310–39.

26. *Apostolic Tradition* 20; see also Cyprian, *Ad Donatum* 5.

27. Everett Ferguson, *Demonology of the Early Christian World* (New York: Edwin Mellen Press, 1984), p. 129. For a similar assessment, see Peter Brown, *The World of Late Antiquity* (London: Thames & Hudson, 1971), p. 55.

28. Thomas M. Finn, "It Happened One Saturday Night: Ritual and Conversion in Augustine's North Africa," *Journal of the American Academy of Religion* 58 (1990): 592.

29. MacMullen, *Christianity and Paganism*, p. 67.

30. Lawrence R. Hennessey, "The Mimesis of Agape in Early Christian Monasticism," in *Nova et Vetera*, ed. John Petruccione (Washington, D.C.: Catholic Univ. of America Press, 1998), p. 147.

31. W. H. C. Frend, "Monks and the End of Greco-Roman Paganism in Syria and Egypt," *Cristianesimo nella storia* 11 (1990): 460–84.

32. David F. Wright, "Augustine and the Transformation of Baptism," in *The Origins of Christendom in the West*, ed. Alan Kreider (Edinburgh: T & T Clark, 2001), pp. 287–312; Paul F. Bradshaw, *Early Christian Worship: A Basic Introduction to Ideas and Practice* (Collegeville, Minn.: Liturgical Press, 1996), chap. 5, "From Adult to Infant Baptism." Bosch mentioned the way in which, in the centuries following Augustine, "the actual performance of the baptismal rite often tended to become more important than the individual's personal appropriation of the faith" (p. 219), which could be a discreet allusion to infant baptism.

33. Kreider, *Worship and Evangelism in Pre-Christendom*, pp. 13–25.

34. Jeff W. Childers, "Refrigerium," in *Encyclopedia of Early Christianity*, ed. Everett Ferguson, rev. ed. (New York: Garland, 1997), 2:275–76.

35. Everett Ferguson, "Catechesis and Initiation," in *Origins of Christendom*, ed. Kreider, pp. 229–68.

36. Neil B. McLynn, *Ambrose of Milan: Church and Court in a Christian Capital* (Berkeley: Univ. of California Press, 1994), p. 255.

37. Peter Brown, *Authority and the Sacred: Aspects of the Christianisation of the Roman World* (Cambridge: Cambridge Univ. Press, 1995), chap. 2.

38. Boniface Ramsey, O.P., "A Note on the Disappearance of the Good Shepherd from Early Christian Art," *Harvard Theological Review* 76 (1983): 365–78.

39. For comment, see Janes, *God and Gold*, pp. 114–15.

40. George H. Williams, "Christology and Church-State Relations in the Fourth Century," *Church History* 20, no. 3 (1951): 12.

41. This ethic can go back to the "two ways" tradition, which is rooted in Psalm 1 and expressed in the *Didache*; in the third century, intimations of what would become the dominant Christendom tradition are found, inter alia, in Origen (*Hom. on Numbers* 25.4; *Contra Celsum* 8.21–23).

42. Edmund Bishop, "Observations on the Liturgy of Narsai," appendix to *The Liturgical Homilies of Narsai*, ed. R. H. Connolly (Cambridge: Cambridge Univ. Press, 1909), pp. 88–93; J. G. Davies, "The Introduction of the Numinous into the Liturgy: An Historical Note," *Studia Liturgica* 8 (1971–72): 216–23.

43. Johannes Quasten, "Mysterium Tremendum: Eucharistische Frömmigkeitsauffassungen des vierten Jahrhunderts," in *Vom Christlichen Mysterium:*

Gesammelte Arbeiten zum Gedächtnis von Odo Casel, O.S.B., ed. A. Mayr, J. Quasten, and B. Neunheuser (Düsseldorf: Patmos, 1951), p. 74; see also Theodor Klauser, *A Short History of the Western Liturgy* (Oxford: Clarendon Press, 1979), pp. 59–63.

44. *Codex Iustinianus* 1.11.10, of 529, in P. R. Coleman-Norton, *Roman State and Christian Church* (London: SPCK, 1966), 3:1048–50.

45. Bosch comments that, by the fourth century, "a Celsus was now by definition unthinkable" (p. 193). Not so; in the fourth century there were still eminent pagan thinkers, including Libanius, Themistius, and Symmachus; and in the 380s there were still vibrant and attractive Jewish communities, such as that in Antioch (Wayne Meeks and Robert Wilken, *Jews and Christians in Antioch in the First Four Centuries of the Common Era* [Missoula, Mont.: Scholars Press, 1978]). That the literary evidence of these non-Christian alternatives has scarcely survived says much about the Christendom tradition of book burning.

46. Richard A. Fletcher, *The Conversion of Europe: From Paganism to Christianity, 371–1386 A.D.* (London: HarperCollins, 1997).

47. Wolfgang Wischmeyer, *Von Golgotha zum Ponte Molle: Studien zur Sozialgeschichte der Kirche im dritten Jahrhundert* (Göttingen: Vandenhoek & Ruprecht, 1992); idem, "The Sociology of Pre-Constantine Christianity," in *Origins of Christendom,* ed. Kreider, pp. 121–52.

48. George W. Horner, ed., *The Statutes of the Apostles; or, Canones Ecclesiastici* (London: Williams & Norgate, 1904), p. 208. For the way that the fourth-century church changed its teaching on warfare, see Alan Kreider, "Military Service in the Church Orders," *Journal of Religious Ethics* 31 (December 2003): 415–42.

49. See John Bolt and Richard A. Muller, "Does the Church Today Need a New 'Mission Paradigm'?" *Calvin Theological Journal* 31 (1996): 196–208; Rodney Clapp, *A Peculiar People: The Church as Culture in a Post-Christian Society* (Downers Grove, Ill.: InterVarsity Press, 1996); Stanley Hauerwas, *After Christendom?* (Nashville: Abingdon Press, 1991).

50. Murray, *Post-Christendom;* David Smith, *Mission After Christendom* (London: Darton, Longman & Todd, 2002).

51. David Smith states: "The further Christendom recedes in our rear-view mirrors, the more relevant the experience of the fathers of the church will be found to be" (*Mission After Christendom,* p. 124).

52. Samuel Hugh Moffett, *A History of Christianity in Asia,* vol. 1, *Beginnings to 1500* (San Francisco: HarperSanFrancisco, 1992); S. P. Brock, "The 'Nestorian' Church: A Lamentable Misnomer," *Bulletin of the John Rylands Library* 78 (1996): 23–35.

53. In parts of Africa "second-century Christianity (and third-century, and even first-century) can still be witnessed and shared in" (Andrew Walls, "Eusebius Tries Again: Reconceiving the Study of Christian History," *International Bulletin of Missionary Research* 24 [July 2000]: 106).

54. Sri Lankan evangelist and missiologist Vinoth Ramachandra concludes

his book *The Recovery of Mission* (Carlisle, Eng.: Paternoster Press, 1996) as follows: "Through humble conversation with the early Christians we shall perhaps discover resources that equip us to face the challenges of interaction with the worldviews and ideologies of our world at the end of the twentieth century, and to bear witness to Jesus Christ with integrity and radicalness" (p. 282). For the use that a gifted Ghanaian theologian is making of the early Christian writers in dialogue with contemporary African societies, see Kwame Bediako, *Theology and Identity: The Impact of Culture upon Christian Thought in the Second Century and in Modern Africa* (Oxford: Regnum Books, 1992).

55. See Philip Jenkins, *The Next Christendom: The Coming of Global Christianity* (New York: Oxford Univ. Press, 2002).

3

New Wineskins for New Wine: Toward a Post-Christendom Ecclesiology

Wilbert R. Shenk

Taking stock of more than a millennium of history, systematic theologian Hendrikus Berkhof asserted, "For centuries a static conception of the church prevailed."[1] Historical Christendom emphasized the institutional and pastoral character of the church. Hierarchical leadership and ecclesiastical tradition reinforced the authority of the church over the members. Theology was preoccupied with the intellectual and pastoral concerns of the church, not its missionary engagement with the world. Mission as intentional witness to the world with a view to winning the allegiance of men and women to the kingdom of God played no direct role in the life of the church of Christendom. When missionary impulses did arise, these were channeled through monastic orders or missionary societies so that the traditional patterns and structures of the church were not disturbed, challenged, or changed. By isolating the question of mission, the church was effectively insulated from the adjustments that missionary engagement inevitably brings.

Since the sixteenth century the missionary movement has contributed to the expansion of the church into the Americas, Asia, Africa, and Oceania, so that the Christian faith has put down roots in a wide variety of cultures and languages. By 1995 at least one book of the Bible had been translated into 2,092 languages, compared with only 60 languages in 1750. The scope and pace of Christian missions accelerated considerably after 1800, setting in motion forces that have reshaped the Christian movement worldwide. This global development demands a rethinking of the nature of the church from every angle: biblical, theological, historical, sociological, and missiological.[2] This work of revision is by no means finished, but significant contributions have already been made. In place of the static and insular model of historical Christendom, it is increasingly acknowledged that only a *missional* church will dynamically engage a changing cultural context effectively.[3]

37

The new ecclesial varieties of this century are emerging from a wide array of linguistic-cultural contexts.[4] We are beginning to recognize that from this diversity of sources we are starting to reap a harvest of new insights and fresh perspectives on the meaning of the Gospel, the varied ways it is being experienced by believers across the world, and the implications this *reformation* holds for the mission of each church. Although it has become commonplace to say that there is no language into which the Bible cannot be translated, we need to recognize that to be credible, the form of the church must engage its cultural-linguistic context in the idiom of that culture.

In this essay I argue that (1) the church was instituted by Jesus Christ for mission; but (2) with the rise of the Constantinian church in the fourth century, mission was eclipsed, and consequently the church became deformed. However, (3) the modern mission movement contributed to the undermining of this nonmissionary model of church by showing that, in the end, missionary action cannot be divorced from the church, for the fruit of authentic mission will be new members of the body of Christ. Finally, (4) the evidence that a church is missional will be the quality of its life.

The Purpose and Constitution of the Church

Although the nature and purpose of the church may seem to be quite straightforward, history shows that it has been understood and interpreted in different ways according to the historical period and the particular social, political, and cultural circumstances. It is essential that we start with the biblical foundation of the church.

According to Scripture the church has been sent into the world by Jesus Christ to continue the witness he began. As such, the church is the primary instrument or means of mission to the world (John 17:18). The church glorifies God by declaring his glory to the nations, calling all people to renounce their idols and turn to the living God, and demonstrating the new reality of the kingdom of God in the way God's people live. Scripture emphasizes that the church has a special responsibility in relation to the world.[5]

Although the church emerges only at Pentecost, its roots can be traced to the calling of the people of God in the Old Testament. The basic pattern is set in Genesis 12:1–3, when God enters into a covenant with Abraham and his descendants: "Now the LORD said to Abram, 'Go from your country and your kindred . . . to the land that I will show you . . .

and I will bless you . . . and in you all the families of the earth shall be blessed." The Abrahamic covenant has been called the original Great Commission. This covenant-commission is foundational for Abraham and the people of God. It becomes clear that God's strategy for redeeming the world is to call out a people that will be the means by which the nations will learn to know and worship God. This strategy is based on the principle of the "one or the few for the many" (i.e., *pars pro toto*).

Since the 1940s certain biblical scholars have argued that the Great Commission that Jesus gave to his disciples following the resurrection is essentially an ecclesiological statement.[6] That is to say, in giving the Great Commission, Jesus renewed the Abrahamic covenant, instituting the church as a primary means of continuing the mission of Jesus in the world (John 17:18; 20:19–23), the one for the many. But the church was not yet ready to be launched. Only after the ascension of Jesus Christ and the coming of the Holy Spirit at Pentecost could the church be called into being. The period between Pentecost and the return of Christ is the age of the Holy Spirit, the time when the church is dispersed throughout the whole world by the Holy Spirit with the mandate to call men and women to believe the Gospel, repent, and live under God's reign.

The Bible interprets the life and meaning of the church primarily through narrative and images that describe the church in living and dynamic terms. When Peter preached at Pentecost (Acts 2), he interpreted what was unfolding at that moment as being in continuity with what God had been doing over the centuries through the patriarchs and prophets. When New Testament writers describe the church, they do so by using images such as people of God, body of Christ, and bride of Christ. Paul S. Minear's classic study *Images of the Church in the New Testament* has greatly enhanced our understanding of the nature of the church.[7] In this book the author identifies ninety-six images used by New Testament writers to describe and define the purpose and functioning of the church. In other words, the Bible relies on word pictures and metaphors to convey to us what the church is and what the church is to do rather than giving us systematic dogmatic formulations.

More recently John Driver extended this line of inquiry by examining these same biblical word pictures from the standpoint of their missiological significance.[8] These images readily cluster into four groups: (1) pilgrimage (the way, sojourners, the poor); (2) new-order (the kingdom of God, new creation, new humanity); (3) peoplehood (the people of God, the family of God, the shepherd and the flock); and (4) transformation (salt and light, a city, a spiritual house, a witnessing community).

Taken together, these images describe the church as a covenant community of missionary witness and transformation that moves throughout the world—God's people among the peoples.

These studies yield two observations. First, the church as the people of God is "set apart" because of its special vocation *on behalf of all other peoples*. There are no people to whom it is not responsible to witness concerning God's saving purpose; the scope of its responsibility is the whole world. Second, the form of the church is not at issue. *No primal form is prescribed* that is to be introduced worldwide. Indeed, it can be said that the church is infinitely translatable or adaptable. The church can be established in every language and culture, taking the form that is appropriate to each particular cultural-linguistic group.

The Church in History

Although there is no consensus among historians as to whether the rise of Constantianism was a positive development or not, they do agree that the church was decisively changed by the decisions taken by Emperor Constantine after A.D. 313 that ultimately led to Christianity being recognized as the official religion of the Roman Empire in 380 under Emperor Theodosius I. Christianity was transformed from a movement located on the margins of society into the official religion of the Roman Empire, from being perceived as a threat to the security of the empire into a guardian of the status quo. Such a profound change in the identity of the church could not fail to have far-reaching implications. Indeed Europe would be known as Christendom until the twentieth century.

It is not our purpose here to evaluate this development. We only note that once Christianity was recognized as the official religion of the empire, it lost its sense of missionary purpose in relation to the world. The nature of evangelization changed. The concern of the rulers was to pacify the European tribes by whatever means necessary. Eventually, the claim was made that lands governed by Christian kings were Christianized, and the notion of territoriality was linked to the meaning of "church."[9] The church was understood to be the institution responsible for the pastoral care of the citizenry and one of the pillars of society. Whereas before A.D. 313 Christians were generally a disadvantaged minority, now as an official part of the establishment, the church played an essential role in the affairs of state.

The long-term consequences of the Constantinian settlement are well known. By the sixteenth century the hierarchy of the church had grown corrupt. The Protestant Reformation challenged certain Catholic practices and doctrines, especially in its great affirmation that sinful humans are "justified by grace alone," not by works. But the Protestant Reformers left intact, among other things, the traditional understanding of how church and state relate, including the assumption that Europe was a Christian culture. Indeed, one of the criticisms leaders of the Counter-Reformation leveled at the Protestant Reformers was that Protestants did not engage in missionary work—meaning sending missionaries from Christendom to other parts of the world.

Some Protestants did engage in evangelization in Europe in the sixteenth century, but only in the seventeenth century did a handful of Protestants begin to initiate missionary outreach beyond Christendom.[10] Since Christendom offered no model of a *missionary* church, these early mission advocates turned to the only existing organizational model of cross-cultural process: the trading company.[11] Starting in the fifteenth century, when the Portuguese and Spanish crowns received authorization from the pope to carry out exploration beyond the borders of Christendom, it became a common practice among European monarchs to grant charters for the establishment of trading companies for the purpose of trade and exploration in other parts of the world. These charters, following the papal precedent, included the requirement that the companies hire chaplains to provide pastoral care of the European employees, along with conducting missionary work among the "heathen." As history shows, the companies allowed the chaplains to perform their pastoral duties among European staff and their families, but they generally discouraged or disallowed them from evangelizing among the indigenous peoples. The Christendom pattern of treating mission as an extraecclesial activity that was permitted only beyond the borders of Christendom persisted among Protestants through the nineteenth century.[12]

Mission and Church Renewal

Already in the seventeenth century concern about the widespread nominality among Protestants was growing. Spiritual life was at low ebb. The Pietist movement arose in Germany in 1675, and in the 1730s the Evangelical Revival started in the Anglo-American world. At each step the official church opposed these efforts to renew the church. Yet Pietism and the Evangelical Revival together were the catalyst for a multifaceted process of renewal that resulted in a range of new initiatives in Christian witness at home and abroad. These many new ventures generated resources for the extension of the church to other parts of the world while instituting a range of new ministries at home—antislavery movement, prison reform, Sunday school movement, literature, Bible societies, and social reforms.

The modern missionary movement emerged around 1800. The immediate evidence that a new initiative was under way was the rapid formation of new missionary agencies in Great Britain, the Netherlands, Germany, and the United States between 1786 and 1825. As quickly as possible these agencies, often with considerable fanfare, began deploying their missionaries to various parts of the world. This movement has contributed substantially to the reshaping of the Christian movement, so that by 1990 more than half of all Christians were to be found beyond the borders of historical Christendom.

What is little appreciated is the way the world mission movement became a leavening influence (some have called it the "blessed reflex") on the so-called sending churches of Europe and North America. In Andrew Walls's telling phrase, the missionary societies aided and abetted "the fortunate subversion of the church."[13] Even though most leaders of Protestant churches in the eighteenth and nineteenth centuries were not prepared to endorse missionary work, the actions of groups of evangelicals—often laypeople—who were committed to foreign missions and a range of domestic philanthropic and evangelistic work became the engine of renewal of the Western church in terms of activity, although not of theology.

Some of the most prominent promoters of foreign missions were men who had been employed by the trading companies or were active in commerce and politics.[14] Using the voluntary society, a legal device introduced into British law around 1700, as the mechanism for recruiting missionaries, raising financial support, and conducting the work, these "enthusiasts" created alternatives to the status quo. In the long term this initiative effectively undermined the ecclesiastical status quo. Over time missionary action exposed a fundamental defect in ecclesiological understanding and practice that kept the church from fulfilling its calling; it also provided a way for pent-up missions enthusiasm to find an outlet.

By the twentieth century the relationship between the churches and missions had changed considerably in terms of formal organizational relationships. The challenge to established modes of thinking came from multiple sources. In addition to the missionary movement that surged ahead during the period 1890–1914, the Pentecostal movement erupted around 1906. Committed to a pneumatically based faith experience and a sense of urgency about world evangelization, in the twentieth century the Pentecostals and the charismatics exerted influence on the wider Christian movement in terms of worship, spirituality, and the role of the laity. Their witness led to a renewed awareness of the work of the Holy Spirit.

Nonetheless, the overshadowing influence of Christendom continued to be felt throughout the Christian church, so that the ecclesiocentric attitude persisted. Notionally, "mission" has remained separate from "church," and "missions" were activities that continued to be carried on through special agencies or programs. In practice, the long-established churches were content to maintain the status quo. The idea that "the church exists by mission as fire by burning" has remained a remote ideal.[15] The process of re-formation cannot yet be said to be complete.

Up to this point we have followed the conventional way of tracing the history of the expansion of the Christian faith. This history starts with the Jerusalem church in A.D. 33 and then follows the spread of the church from the Mediterranean region into Europe. It then moves northward across Europe. From Europe the faith crosses the Atlantic to North and South America. It continues spreading to all the other continents from this European base. The entire Christian movement can be linked genealogically to one church or the other in the West. But an important corrective is needed if we are to give a more adequate account of what has happened since 1800.

Spread across the world today is another variety of church: the indigenous Christian movement. This is not a united movement but rather a conglomeration, for these movements started locally with leaders drawn from their own ranks. Nonetheless, these indigenous groups do owe something to the Christian missions. The coming of the missions inevitably set up an encounter with the local cultures and traditional religions that sparked response.[16] Some people became Christians and affiliated with the churches that were organized by missionaries, while others accepted the message the missionary brought but declined to join the "missionary" church with its foreign connotations. From the beginning, relations between mission-founded churches and indigenous churches were troubled. Whether one considers groups like the True Jesus Church and Little Flock in China or the many indigenous churches in Africa, the mission-related churches generally treated the indigenous groups with contempt mixed with suspicion. And the indigenous churches reciprocated in kind.

While the two groups share a common indebtedness to missionary initiative, presence, and witness, they have also been separated by a profound difference. The indigenous groups did not start from a formal relationship with missionary agencies; they have never experienced dependency on an outside agency or body. From the beginning, they have chosen to pursue Christian faith in their own way, adapting the Christian message to their context as seemed good to them. They have developed their own hymnody, church structures and polity, and theological identity. In other words, these indigenous churches, all of which have emerged since 1800, represent many new varieties of church.

At this point our conventional understanding of the church needs to be challenged. It is generally assumed that once a local church is established, as a self-sufficient entity it can be expected to grow and function as a viable expression of the body of Christ. The energies of the sponsoring church can be devoted continually to establishing new churches. But actual experience shows that this assumption must be questioned, for it fails to take into account an important issue: church growth dare not be separated from church renewal. The seeds of decay are present in every local church, no matter how healthy it appears to be. What is needed is an ecclesiology that addresses both dimensions by holding church *growth* in tension with church *renewal*. A *missional* ecclesiology attempts to do this.

Missional Ecclesiology

The quest for a new ecclesial vision will not be realized easily. The inertia of the old form is formidable. The new will come to birth only through struggle. It will involve a conversion in our understanding of the church and the role of the church in the world.

Mission the test of faith. Without mission the church dies. Although what we ordinarily call the church may continue to exist as a religious group, a missionless church is no longer an authentic church. The proof of its missionary character will be demonstrated by its response to the world. W. A. Visser 't Hooft proposed that missionary witness is a test of Christian faith and ecclesial reality because of three requirements:

- In the missionary situation the church must demonstrate that it actually believes in the "happenedness" of what God has done in Jesus Christ.
- In the missionary situation the church must declare whether it believes in the universal claims of the Gospel.
- In the missionary situation the church must affirm that God's

Word is not bound to any one culture, and especially not to Western cultural forms.[17]

These requirements put the church on notice that it carries special responsibilities in relation to both God and the world. No other body or religious group is defined by these three criteria. When the church no longer makes these affirmations, it has changed character and has forfeited its distinctive purpose.

Today we have grounds for believing that we can look forward to the flowering of a missional ecclesiology in the twenty-first century, for we have resources that hitherto were not available. The growth of the church throughout the world over the past two centuries has had a twofold effect. First, this development has decisively relativized the historical ecclesial model inherited from Christendom by showing that it belongs to a particular historical period. Second, this growth has occurred in a vast array of cultures and peoples where there was no church in 1800, which has opened our eyes to a conceptual and theological richness not recognized before. Furthermore, the authenticity of these newer expressions of Christian faith has been tested by persistent opposition and, frequently, in the fires of persecution. With the collapse of historical Christendom, the church today is a minority in most countries. To be viable the church must assume a *missionary* relationship to every culture.

Mission and the signs of the time. Mission is the means by which God is restoring humankind to God's original purpose in creation. Mission gives history a goal, namely, the realization of the kingdom of God. The present age of the Spirit is marked by intense conflict between the kingdom of God and the kingdom of the world. Mark 13 outlines the nature of this conflict and the way the church is implicated in it.[18] We can make four observations about the role of mission in this "end time." First, the witness to the Gospel will take place in a situation of claims and counterclaims. Many pretenders will proclaim themselves to be messiah, but these false messiahs cannot deliver what they promise (Mark 13:6, 21–22). Messianic options can also take the form of ideologies and revolutionary movements that claim they will liberate humankind from its present dilemma. The people of God must engage in careful discernment of the times under the guidance of the Holy Spirit. Unless the church is clear and convincing in its testimony, its witness will be confused and ineffective.

Second, the kingdom of the world will mount intense opposition, including resort to tactics of intimidation and physical abuse, but nothing must be allowed to stand in the way of witness "to all nations" (Mark 13:9–10) that Jesus is the Messiah. The church dare not make the mistake of thinking that it must gain control of society in order to proclaim the Gospel. God has not called the church to govern the world but to witness to God's plan to renew the world based on the justice/righteousness of God. There is no part of this world to which God has relinquished claim. God has ceded no territory or people to the control of Satan. That is why witness to the Gospel must be carried to the whole world. This claim is of course contested, and those who witness to the lordship of Jesus the Messiah will inevitably be called to suffer.

Third, the missional church will not lose sight of the fact that the mission does not belong to the church. Mission is the work of the Holy Spirit, who indwells the church. As Mark's gospel reminds us, "Whenever you are arrested and brought to trial, do not worry beforehand about what to say. Just say whatever is given you at the time, for it is not you speaking, but the Holy Spirit" (Mark 13:11 NIV). The missional church will be acutely aware that it is the instrument the Spirit is using to accomplish the mission of Jesus.

Finally, in spite of the threats the world will inevitably hurl at the church, it will quietly draw confidence from the conviction that God alone will determine the outcome (Mark 13:32b).

Missional ecclesiology tested. We can learn from the experiences of Christian disciples who have demonstrated a strong sense of missionary purpose in their particular situations at various times over the past two thousand years. The two examples cited here have not been chosen because they report on perfect churches. Rather, what we want to illustrate is what has been the instinctual faith-response of a missional church to its historical-cultural context.

In the first case we actually know little of the church(es) being described, but the description suggests a church that exhibited an authentic missional ethos. The *Letter to Diognetus,* believed to have come down to us from the second century, characterizes a particular Christian community:

> Christians are not differentiated from other people by country, language or customs; you see, they do not live in cities of their own, or speak some strange dialect, or have some peculiar lifestyle.
> They live in both Greek and foreign cities, wherever chance has put them. They follow local customs in clothing, food and the other aspects of

life. But at the same time, they demonstrate to us the wonderful and certainly unusual form of their own citizenship.

They live in their own native lands, but as aliens; as citizens, they share all things with others; but like aliens suffer all things. Every foreign country is to them as their native country, and every native land as a foreign country.

They are treated outrageously and behave respectfully to others. When they do good, they are punished as evildoers; when punished, they rejoice as if being given new life. They are attacked by Jews as aliens, and are persecuted by Greeks; yet those who hate them cannot give any reason for their hostility.

To put it simply—the soul is to the body as Christians are to the world. The soul is spread through all parts of the body and Christians through all the cities of the world. The soul is in the body but is not of the body; Christians are in the world but not of the world.[19]

The Meserete Kristos Church (MK) in Ethiopia provides us with a contemporary example. In 1982 the Communist government singled out this church for persecution by sealing all the MK church buildings and forbidding the holding of church services. The main leaders of the church were put in prison, but the members of the church responded quickly. They worked out a plan by which the entire church was organized into house groups. Services had to be held in secret. Since there was always the possibility of a police raid, such things as hymnbooks were not brought to the meetings. The number of members in each group was limited so as not to attract attention. Women took charge of many of these groups. New converts were baptized in secret. Sunday school materials were produced and distributed. Communication among MK congregations was strictly by word of mouth, lest written documents fall into the hands of government officials. The ban against the Meserete Kristos Church was not lifted until the Communist government was overthrown in 1991. As happened in China during the years 1949–79, the Meserete Kristos Church grew during the years of persecution. In 1982 baptized membership was reported to be 27,440. When the ban was lifted in 1991, membership had risen to 48,056.[20] The MK has continued growing in the years since.

Defining characteristics. What can we say are the main features of a missional ecclesiology? At least five things will characterize a missional church:

- The missional church is intensely aware that its priority is to witness to the kingdom of God so that people are being liberated from the oppressive power of idols. The church is consciously discerning and naming the idols.

- The church is deeply committed to the world but is not controlled by the world. In other words, the church knows that it has been placed in the world but is never to be subservient to the world. The absence of this tension indicates that the church has made its peace with the world.
- Mission is patterned after the example of Jesus the Messiah; that is, mission is cruciform. The vision of Isaiah 53 is being fulfilled as God's people *serve* and *witness*. The cross is central.
- The missional church has a keen awareness of the *eschaton*. In Jesus Christ the kingdom has been inaugurated, but the people of God eagerly await the consummation of the kingdom.
- Church structures will serve and support its mission to the world. Human cultures inevitably change over time. The church must stay abreast of its changing cultural context, which will require the dismantling of archaic forms that impede missionary witness and the devising of new structures that support the mission.

Conclusion

When our Lord launched his earthly ministry, he called individuals to follow him. Questions were soon raised about the way the disciples of Jesus, in contrast to those of John the Baptist, were departing from traditional practice with regard to fasting. Jesus responded by interpreting his ministry in new terms. A new age was dawning, he said, in which the old rules no longer made sense. To clarify this point Jesus told two parables. He said the sensible person does not tear a piece of cloth off a new garment and use it to patch a hole in an old one; likewise, it is foolish to pour new wine into an old wineskin (Matt. 9:14–17; Mark 2:18–22; Luke 5:33–39). In effect, said Jesus, we must pay attention to what God the Holy Spirit is doing in a particular time and place. Forms and practices are not sacrosanct. The action of the triune God expressed as *missio Dei* is authoritative in determining what the people of God do.

The thrust of this essay has been to argue that the ecclesiology inherited from Christendom has been marked by a twofold distortion: (1) Christendom ecclesiology is nonmissional, and (2) it has been regarded as permanently normative. I have contended that the New Testament leaves no doubt as to the fundamental purpose of the church but does not prescribe the polity or form of the church. As the primitive church began spreading around the Mediterranean basin and into Asia, issues arose as to theology, ethics, and missionary engagement. Paul forged his theology in the thick of missionary witness. In his epistles to these new churches, the apostle grapples with the issues being raised in the context of Christian expansion into new cultures. At no point does he address the problem of structure and form. Rather, he focuses on matters of Christian commitment and discipleship.

When we turn to examples from history where churches have shown authentic spiritual vitality, we observe that such churches have been marked by a strong sense of their identity as the body of Christ engaged in faithful witness to the world. To carry out this witness has invariably required new structures and forms appropriate to the cultural context. Old wineskins cannot handle new wine.

Over the past two centuries the modern mission movement has been the instrument for extending the church to all parts of the world. The cultural variety that marks the worldwide church today is without historical precedent. As the Gospel has penetrated these diverse cultures, it has yielded this extraordinary fruit. The Gospel is the pearl of great price that no human can ever fully comprehend. At best we grasp only a part of the Gospel. By the same token, the way the Gospel is heard and appropriated by any local church will reflect its cultural and linguistic particularities.[21] What validates these diverse expressions of Christian faith is the vitality of the witness of each church in its own context.

Notes

1. Hendrikus Berkhof, *Christian Faith* (Grand Rapids: Eerdmans, 1979), pp. 411–12.
2. The pioneering work by Lesslie Newbigin, *The Household of God* (New York: Friendship Press, 1954), shows how ecclesiology must be rethought from the standpoint of the church's missionary purpose.
3. The term "missional" has been used increasingly since the 1990s. However, already in the mid-1970s John Howard Yoder began teaching a course, "Ecclesiology in Missional Perspective," at the Associated Mennonite Biblical Seminary. "Missional" describes the church defined by its relationship to the *missio Dei*, or mission of God. "Missiology" refers to the process of systematic study of missionary action. For a recent attempt to rethink ecclesiology from a missional perspective, see Darrell L. Guder, ed., *Missional Church: A Vision for the Sending of the Church in North America* (Grand Rapids: Eerdmans, 1998). Note that this book develops a missional ecclesiology in relation to a particular cultural context.
4. See Sunday Babajide Komolafe, "The Changing Face of Christianity: Revisiting African Creativity," *Missiology* 32, no. 2 (April 2004), for a

stimulating study of the repeated emergence of new varieties of church in Nigeria since 1846, but with emphasis on the twentieth century.

5. Inagrace T. Dietterich, *The Church and the Reign of God* (Chicago: Center for Parish Development, 2002), suggests that five things characterize the church: (1) the church was founded at God's initiative, not by human decision; (2) the church's God-given mission is threefold: to be *sign, foretaste,* and *instrument* of the coming kingdom of God; (3) the church is called to discern and participate in God's vision of the future, not a program of the church's own devising; (4) the church is called to continual renewal of its life and ministry around the "new thing" that God is doing (Isa. 43:19); and (5) each local church must discover the orientation for its life in terms of two processes: discerning God's vision and discerning God's call (pp. 2–3).

6. E.g., Otto Michel, "The Conclusion of Matthew's Gospel: A Contribution to the History of the Easter Message," in *The Interpretation of Matthew,* ed. Graham Stanton (Philadelphia: Fortress Press, 1983), pp. 30–41 (first published in German in 1941); David J. Bosch, "The Structure of Mission: An Exposition of Matthew 28:16–20," in *Exploring Church Growth,* ed. Wilbert R. Shenk (Grand Rapids: Eerdmans, 1983), pp. 218–48.

7. Paul S. Minear, *Images of the Church in the New Testament* (Philadelphia: Westminster, 1960).

8. John Driver, *Images of the Church in Mission* (Scottdale, Pa.: Herald Press, 1997).

9. Not until the Protestant Reformation was the principle *cujus regio, ejus religio* formalized. Such a principle was the logical outcome of the foundational concept forged by Constantine and Theodosius I.

10. See David J. Bosch, *Transforming Mission* (Maryknoll, N.Y.: Orbis Books, 1991), pp. 245–48, for one discussion. The most complete survey of the period 1500–1800 remains Kenneth Scott Latourette, *A History of the Expansion of Christianity: Three Centuries of Advance, A.D. 1500–1800* (New York: Harper & Brothers, 1939).

11. For one study, see William Kellaway, *The New England Company, 1649–1776* (London: Longmans, 1961).

12. Official Roman Catholic teaching continues to maintain this definition. See John Paul II's encyclical *Redemptoris missio* (Washington, D.C.: U.S. Catholic Conference, 1990), sections 34 and 37. Some ambivalence is evident in this restatement of traditional teaching.

13. From the title of chapter 18 of Andrew F. Walls, *The Missionary Movement in Christian History* (Maryknoll, N.Y.: Orbis Books, 1996).

14. Perhaps the best-known example was the Clapham Sect, so named because this group of men and their families lived in Clapham, South London, between 1785 and 1815. This group comprised prominent bankers, lawyers, members of Parliament, and merchants who were also convinced evangelical Anglicans. Included in their number were Charles Grant, a leading director of the East India Company; William Wilberforce, merchant and member of Parliament; and Zachary Macaulay, governor of the Sierra Leone Company

in the 1790s. The Clapham Sect supported many of the new evangelical societies that sponsored foreign missions and philanthropy at home.
15. Emil Brunner, *The Word and the World* (London: SCM Press, 1931), p. 108.
16. Based on his unparalleled knowledge of these movements worldwide, Harold W. Turner argued this point repeatedly. See his article "Religious Movements in Primal (or Tribal) Societies," *Mission Focus* 9, no. 3 (September 1983): 45–55.
17. In Ronald K. Orchard, ed., *Witness in Six Continents* (London: Edinburgh House Press, 1964), pp. 23–24.
18. This section draws on Lesslie Newbigin, *Trinitarian Faith and Today's Mission* (Richmond, Va.: John Knox Press, 1964), pp. 38–46.
19. Tim Dowley, ed., *Eerdmans' Handbook to the History of Christianity* (Grand Rapids: Eerdmans, 1977), p. 69.
20. Between 1991 and 1994 membership increased from 48,056 to 62,445. Grateful acknowledgment is made of this information supplied by Tesfatsion C. Dalellew, a former executive secretary of the Meserete Kristos Church, in personal communications January 22 and Feb-ruary 19, 2004.
21. See John V. Taylor, *The Growth of the Church in Buganda* (London: SCM, 1958), pp. 252–53. Taylor approaches the issue as "a question of communication" and brilliantly illustrates how missionaries and Bugandans talked past each other, even though both were responding to the Gospel, and how a strong church emerged among the Buganda. In 1884–85 persecution of Christians broke out, and in early 1885 three young men sealed their faith in death. Persecution against the Christian community continued, but the church only grew in strength.

4

Conflicting Understandings of Christian Conversion: A Missiological Challenge

Richard V. Peace

We are seeing today a lively interest in Christian conversion, which perhaps reflects the fascination North American culture has had with spirituality since the 1990s.[1] That interest arose, not coincidentally, just as the baby-boomer generation started passing through midlife, a time of increased interest in the meaning of life. This interest in spirituality and conversion has continued unabated into the new millennium, fueled by the needs and interests of both Generation X and the millennial generation.

In the New Testament the word *epistrophe* (conversion) means turning around—that is, reversing direction and going the opposite way. One turns from the way of sin to the way of Jesus. The other key New Testament term, *metanoia* (repentance), also conveys the idea of turning, but it focuses on the inner, cognitive decision to make a break with the past. *Metanoia* must be combined with *pistis* (faith) in order to bring about *epistrophe* (as in the summary in Mark 1:15 of Jesus' message). So when Paul describes to King Agrippa what he preached to Jew and Gentile, he says it is "that they should repent and turn to God and do deeds consistent with repentance" (Acts 26:20). Christian conversion is characterized by a decision (repentance) based on understanding (awareness, consciousness, conviction) to turn around from a life of sin (darkness, disobedience, waywardness) to the way of Jesus (light, God, holiness), with a resultant new way of living in the context of the kingdom of God. In theological terms, conversion is the human experience of salvation (vs. the inner reality of regeneration, which is the hidden work of God).[2]

The most famous example of conversion in the New Testament is Paul's turning on the Damascus road. This experience is so central to the New Testament (where it is related three times in the Book of Acts and referred to by Paul in four major texts) and to the church (from it the mission to the Gentiles emerged, which ultimately led to the Western church and much of the missionary movement) that it has become for many people the paradigm of true conversion.[3]

Once we move beyond this biblical definition into the world of the church, however, we encounter different understandings of what constitutes genuine Christian conversion. Disputes among the various branches of the Christian family have erupted as one view of conversion has been used to argue against the legitimacy of all competing views. One's view of conversion is significant, however, for it shapes and determines one's view of evangelism. This matter therefore has deep missiological significance.

In this article I consider the way conversion is understood in five major Christian traditions: evangelical, Pentecostal, mainline Protestant, Roman Catholic, and Orthodox. For purposes of this exploration, I use the typology for conversion suggested by Scot McKnight, who speaks of "three basic orientations to conversion: socialization, liturgical acts, and personal decision." He notes that "each is aligned with a major component of the church, and each appears to be allergic to the others. Evangelicals worry about Roman Catholic conversions; Roman Catholics are uneasy with evangelical conversion; mainline denominations are uncomfortable with both; on the rebound, evangelicals and Roman Catholics lift their eyebrows at mainline Christianity. . . . These groups squabble and feud with one another, usually politely but sometimes polemically."[4] We consider these orientations in reverse order.

Conversion Through Personal Decision

Evangelicals. I begin with evangelicals because conversion has been central in this tradition, both in its self-identity and in its practice of ministry. I include in this group both fundamentalists and charismatics, since they share with evangelicals a common understanding of conversion, though with differences in practice and in certain theological positions.

Within the evangelical world, conversion is a defining emphasis. One cannot be considered a Christian unless one has been converted—and the more like Paul's Damascus road experience, the better. This kind of conversion is a sudden, punctiliar event, triggered by an encounter of some sort (with truth, with Jesus, with conviction of sin, with the plan of salvation, etc.) that marks the beginning point of the Christian life.

The strength of this perspective is its simplicity and functionality. Salvation becomes a matter of believing certain doctrines, trusting Jesus for forgiveness, and praying a prayer of commitment. Conversion is an individual experience that can be dated exactly. This view of conversion also provides laypeople with a concrete way by which to be witnesses for Jesus. They simply need to memorize a "plan of salvation" and share it with others.[5] It is all quite well organized, simple, specific, and understandable.

Understanding conversion to be a matter of a personal decision effected by simple belief and prayer has resulted in countless men and women who have started to follow Jesus. The growth of many national churches around the world can be traced back to this perspective on conversion. It has generated the many evangelistic ministries with which we are familiar: mass evangelism, door-to-door visitation, tract distribution in public places, and many others.[6]

Unfortunately, a large percentage of these conversions are later abandoned. For example, Donald Miller noted in connection with the Harvest Crusades of evangelist Greg Laurie: "Greg Laurie's staff estimates that 16,000 conversions occurred at Harvest Christian Fellowship in the five-year period from 1986 to 1991. . . . Perhaps only 10 percent of these decisions resulted in long-term changes in personal behavior."[7] This is a stunning statistic but not much different from what one hears informally from other evangelical evangelists. Such "erosion" raises the question of the validity of this personalistic definition of conversion. Can genuine Christian conversion regularly occur via a presentation of the "facts of gospel" that are believed and affirmed by a "sinner's prayer"? Evangelical missions must wrestle with this question.

My own sense, based on years of experience in evangelical evangelism both in North America and abroad, is that while conversion can indeed take place in such circumstances, it is by no means as automatic or certain as evangelicals teach or imply.[8] Biblically, the real challenge for the church is to make disciples (i.e., those who are actively and consciously following the way of Jesus), not to make converts (those who take a tentative first step toward Jesus). For evangelical missions, evangelism and spiritual formation need to be relinked. Much can be learned from both liturgical and socialization traditions of conversion that can aid in this process of making disciples by connecting them to communities and to worship rather than leaving converts to find their own way in the Christian life.

There are additional weaknesses in the decisionist tradition. In many cases this "technology of conversion" leaves potential converts frustrated, bewildered, and angry. "I tried it, but it didn't work. Christianity is not for me." Could it be that our evangelistic efforts result too often in immunizing people against Christianity, with only minimal positive results? Is evangelism really meant to be a matter of percentages: the more people contacted, the more converted, without regard to the vast number of people alienated by this process?

Another weakness is that such a perspective often fails to recognize that genuine conversion takes place in a variety of ways. For example, research indicates that no more than 30 percent of all conversions are punctiliar in nature. Most conversions take place over time, often with many fits and starts as one moves toward Jesus and his way. For most people, conversion is a process, not an event.[9] Paul's conversion is not the only paradigm for conversion in the New Testament. In the Gospel of Mark we have the story of the unfolding conversion process of the Twelve, which gives us another way of thinking about conversion and doing evangelism.

Pentecostals. The Pentecostal view of conversion is similar to a traditional evangelical view, namely, that conversion takes place when an individual turns from sin to Jesus via repentance and faith and so receives Jesus as Lord and Savior. In many places, however, the Pentecostal view leads to a greater fervor in seeking to lead others to conversion. Evangelicals may have the same beliefs about conversion, but often it does not lead to an impassioned outreach ministry, whereas Pentecostal groups (especially in the Two-Thirds World) tend to practice continuous outreach involving every member. This evangelistic fervor comes from an eschatological urgency that insists that time is short—the Lord may return, or you may die—so decide for Jesus today!

Furthermore, Pentecostal conversions are typically more intense than those experienced by evangelicals. Evangelical conversion can be solely cerebral, merely a matter of believing a few things and praying a simple prayer. Pentecostal conversion, in contrast, is often accompanied by signs of power that convince converts that God is immediately active and present in their lives. Especially in the Two-Thirds World, so-called power evangelism is a potent force for conversion.[10]

Conversion Through Socialization

Mainline Protestants. McKnight asserts, "For many Christians conversion is a process of socialization."[11] From this perspective, Christianity is a matter more of nurture than of decision; the key decision is made on behalf of individuals as parents bring their infant children for baptism. The decision later required of these baptized children when they become adults has more to do with continuing alignment with the community than with following Jesus. The key activities of postbaptism nurture in mainline churches are Sunday school instruction (for children), catechism and confirmation (for teens), and active participation in church leadership (for adults). In a mainline Protestant context people may be uncomfortable speaking about "becoming a Christian." It is more natural to talk about "being a Christian."

In his helpful article "The Mainline Protestant Understanding of Conversion," Donald McKim lists eight theological images of conversion.[12] One image is that of *transition*, as in the theology of Horace Bushnell: if children are nurtured in the Christian faith, they will never know themselves as anything other than Christians. Today's mainline church no longer holds a single view of conversion, nor is the operative view of conversion based on Reformation theology. Rather, it emerges from whatever central image captivates a particular congregation or denomination. Those who are guided by the image of liberation theology, for example, would understand conversion differently from those whose focus is feminist theology.

In point of fact, I find that mainline churches generally display a curious reluctance to talk about conversion at all.[13] It is almost as if members believed that the word itself has been co-opted by other theological traditions and thus is not to be used because it connotes something with which we are uncomfortable. "Conversion" may be viewed as a power word, with those who use it seeking domination over others, defining for others what their experience must be. In addition, in mainline churches there is a kind of delicacy to inquiring about conversion, almost as if to raise the question is to suggest that some might be converted and others not.

In such a context it is easy enough to allow conversion and the work of conversion (i.e., evangelism) to drift from the center of one's ecclesiastical vision, as I think it has for many mainline churches. Significant amounts of money, though, have been spent in recent years in mainline denominations to promote the work of evangelism. For example, an independent fund within the United Methodist Church pays for professors of evangelism in Methodist seminaries. Mainline denominations have offices of evangelism that produce literature and seminars. Resolutions about evangelism are passed in Synod meetings. Unfortunately, though, nothing much gets done, largely because of a reluctance to put conversion into the center of our theological horizon.

There is a difference among church members, with some seeming to have a vital faith, and others what must be described as a nominal faith. Gordon Allport noted this difference in his seminal work on racial prejudice, in which he distinguished between those whose faith is intrinsic and those whose faith is extrinsic.[14] For the former, faith is alive, real, and personal; for the latter, it is more a matter of form, duty, tradition, and obligation. The challenge for the mainline church is to help members move from extrinsic faith (nominalism) to intrinsic faith (inner conviction). This change is a kind of conversion in itself.

Mainline churches need to help their membership commit themselves consciously to what is implicit in church activity and membership. Without such consciousness, church membership becomes like club membership: you hang out with nice people, but when you go home, such membership makes little difference in your life and the lives of others. We need to create ways for people to grow in all aspects of faith: belief, commitment, service, relationships, justice, spirituality, and more.

Nominalism is the danger in the new paradigm in North American evangelism expressed by the dictum "belonging before believing."[15] This evangelistic strategy—invite people into the community first, and in that context tell them about Jesus—is commendable. I believe it rescues evangelism from the highly individualistic tone it has often assumed in North America, for it puts belief in Jesus in the context of the community of Jesus. It rescues conversion from being a kind of legalistic insurance policy that guarantees heaven and allows it, instead, to become incorporation into the kingdom of God in the here and now. The danger of this perspective, however, is that it calls people to community without sufficient focus on what it means to be a child of God whose primary allegiance is to Jesus. Faith in Jesus needs to be internalized in order to be real.

Conversion Through Liturgical Acts

McKnight refers to mainline Christians as "socialized converts," and he imagines them asking "liturgical converts" why so much attention is given to baptism, the Eucharist, and "official rites of passage."[16] And indeed also for "personal-decision converts," the focus on sacraments is difficult to understand. How can one be converted without experiencing conversion or community, these other Christians ask?

Roman Catholics. Catholic reflection on conversion is caught between the experience of Augustine and the fact of infant baptism. Is conversion an experience, or is it a grace mediated by the church? For Augustine, conversion came in a moment when he heard a voice telling him to pick up the New Testament and read. As he did, "there was infused in my heart something like the light of full certainty and all the gloom of doubt vanished away."[17]

There is an interesting body of literature dealing with conversion in the Roman Catholic Church, shaped in particular by the writings of Bernard Lonergan.[18] Contemporary Catholic writing insists that "conversion cannot be isolated and reduced to a self-conscious moment."[19] Yet it is aware of the problem when the subjective (experiential) element of conversion is removed or muted. Karl Rahner is "concerned that the administration of the sacraments in the average parish often 'masked' the experience of conversion behind baptism, confirmation, and first communion."[20] Rahner goes on to encourage Catholics to give up their suspicion of "the conversion phenomenon" and embrace the whole idea of conscious conversion.

When conversion is the outcome of a ritual that is entered into for a variety of reasons—custom, expectation, family, convenience, social status, as well as genuine faith—it can result in nominal faith.[21] "I am a Catholic because I was born a Catholic and baptized a Catholic." Even though the ritual itself is filled with meaning and power, that meaning and power can be sapped (in the here and now at least) by the motives and responses of those participating in the ritual. In the same way that "praying the sinner's prayer" (in the evangelical context) or "joining the church" (in the mainline context) can be mechanical and devoid of real content and meaning, so too can one's baptism be empty in liturgical churches. In each instance the challenge is to help the convert move from the event or the experience into a genuine discipleship.

The Catholic Church recognizes the problem because of the defining power for them of Augustine's *experience* of conversion. Their challenge is to maintain a sacramental view of theology while emphasizing the experiential side of conversion. The Rite of Christian Initiation of Adults is a movement within the Catholic Church that seeks to promote the process of conversion.

Orthodox. Though similar to the Roman Catholic Church in its strong, priest-centered, liturgically oriented community, the Orthodox Church has been more closely tied to ethnic identity. A recent article on the character of Orthodox churches in the United States thus identifies the various branches of the church by their regional origin: Greek Orthodox, Serbian Orthodox, Russian Orthodox, Romanian Orthodox, Bulgarian Orthodox, Ethiopian Orthodox, and so forth.[22] In speaking of the addition of church members, Archbishop Paul of Finland has said, "Nowadays people become members of the Church in infancy through Holy Baptism."[23] This comment well expresses the family-oriented, community-based nature of much of Orthodoxy. The strong tie between the church and ethnic communities means that much of the growth is what could be called biological growth. Outreach to others beyond one's ethnic community has not been a high priority in many Orthodox churches.

Adults wishing to join the Orthodox Church are encouraged to attend an Orthodox church so as to become familiar with the services and how to take part in them. Then, in due course, they are baptized and undergo chrismation, a sacrament similar to confirmation. Once baptized, such a person is a member of God's family, which is the key issue. "However careless and indifferent the baptized may be in their subsequent life, this indwelling presence of the Spirit is never totally withdrawn. But unless [they] co-operate with God's grace . . . it is likely that the Spirit's presence within [them] will remain hidden and unconscious."[24]

Salvation is found in the church. Ware quotes approvingly the assertion by Aleksei Khomiakov: "No one is saved alone. He who is saved is saved in the Church, as a member of her and in union with all her other members." In other words, salvation is ecclesial. Ware adds that salvation is also sacramental, for in the sacraments a person is made one with God.[25] In this same vein, Alexander Schmemann asserts that the mission of the Orthodox Church is found in Word and sacrament. To celebrate the liturgy is to be the kingdom of God; to experience the liturgy is to experience God. "The sacrament is a manifestation of the Word. . . . This is why the reading and preaching of the Gospel in the Orthodox Church is a liturgical act, an integral and essential part of the sacrament."[26] Certainly the apostle Paul would seem to support this view, when he writes, "For as often as you eat this bread and drink the cup, you proclaim the Lord's death until he comes" (1 Cor. 11:26).

The word "conversion" does not seem to be part of the functional vocabulary in the Orthodox Church.[27] It is not that Orthodoxy is uninterested in conversion, salvation, justification, or sanctification but that it talks about these realities in a different way. Only when one reads the small but growing missiological literature in the Orthodox Church does one begin to hear more familiar words and phrases.[28] "The main task of mission is the conversion of those outside the Church. . . . Thus preaching is preaching with a purpose, that people might believe and be converted. 'Conversion' is the proper word to use, since those who are outside the Church need to be introduced to the grace of God in Christ.

Yet mission is not just to the outsider but also 'the way in which Church people . . . try to arouse the sleeping faith of the nominal Christian.'"[29]

Orthodox evangelism has a different tone to it, however. As John Meyendorff states in his introduction to James Stamoolis's book, "A church can be 'witnessing' and therefore preaching through its prayer, through its sense of being 'different' from the surrounding society, and through its celebration of the Kingdom of God, present, by anticipation, in the liturgy. The way the Orthodox have succeeded in experiencing their worship as communion with the risen Body of Christ, and in using it as a powerful educational tool, is probably the most distinctive trait of Eastern Christianity, in contrast to the Western tendency of identifying mission with activism and organization."[30] In this view, liturgy itself is the method of evangelism.

Thus the challenge for the Orthodox Church is to invite people convincingly to come into the service of worship; to learn the service and how to participate in it, and so to prepare themselves to be baptized and join the Orthodox Church in order to participate in the mysteries of Christ. In this age of fascination with the spiritual, the Orthodox way will have great appeal to many. It rings of mystery, which is engraved in the buildings themselves, displayed in the multiple icons, and demonstrated in the liturgy. Those from nonliturgical traditions have much to learn about the power of mystery and the appeal of community as we seek to reach out to this current age.

The downside of this approach is the same as for the Roman Catholic Church: when the meaning of ritual is lost, one faces the risk of nominalism. Hence the call in the Orthodox missiological literature to wake the sleeping faith of nominal Christians.

Summation

So who is right? Who has understood accurately the nature of Christian conversion? Who has translated this understanding into an effective ministry of evangelism? Is conversion a matter of making a decision for Jesus? Or joining a church? Or being baptized?

I hope that my position, implied in the discussion so far, is clear: *no single view captures fully the nature of conversion.* All views contribute important parts to a holistic understanding of conversion and hence of evangelism. Holistic evangelism will invite people into the kingdom of God. It will invite them to turn to Jesus in repentance and faith in the context of the community of God's people, which has worship and the sacraments at its center. Such evangelism will invite nominal Christians to become active followers of Jesus. It will engage genuine seekers as they explore the issues that will move them forward in their pilgrimages. It will not settle for cultural faith. It will have as its goal the genuine conversion of others, even as the evangelists themselves continue their own conversion process.[31]

The Missiological Challenge

While we can and should learn from one another when it comes to conversion, in fact there is much suspicion between Christian traditions over the issue of conversion. For example, evangelicals feel quite free to seek converts from the Orthodox Church in Russia because, in their eyes, the Orthodox are not real Christians and need to be converted. For their part, the Orthodox in America are quite open to receiving new members from other churches because their church is the one true church. Those outside Orthodoxy are schismatics who need to return home to the real church.[32] Mainline Christians are suspicious of all talk of conversion and so resist efforts at conversion, whether these originate from without (proselytizing) or even from within their own denomination (sponsored by denominational evangelism commissions). Roman Catholics are baffled when they see fellow Catholics leaving to join a nondenominational charismatic church that is unconnected to historic Christianity.

Given this situation, there is some urgency to expand our understanding of conversion. Our suspicions of one another impede the real task of evangelism, which is to proclaim Christ to those who do not know his name or follow his way.

Is there not a common core of understanding about conversion upon which we can all build? I suggest the following:

1. The real question when it comes to Christian conversion is conscious commitment to Jesus (by repentance and faith). Such a commitment is expressed in a variety of ways—through belief, via baptism and confirmation, in membership and participation in a Christian community, through participation in the sacraments. In the end, *conversion is about the human experience of God's saving grace*—awareness, consciousness, commitment, deliberately turning one's life around, coming to a whole new understanding of what life is all about.
2. *Nominalism is an issue in all Christian denominations.* Thus the challenge for all churches is to have in place a vigorous program

of spiritual formation with the aim of encouraging ongoing spiritual pilgrimage so that nominal faith will grow into vital faith. Can we not assist one another in such formational activities rather than poaching each other's members?

3. Different denominations emphasize different issues: belief, liturgy, or membership. The challenge is to *recognize and build upon the evangelistic opportunities that each emphasis affords.* For example, in Orthodox missiological literature, the evangelistic nature of the Great Liturgy is recognized and promoted. And in mainline churches with rich and powerful community in place, can we not with deliberation work at inviting others into this community? Evangelicals have much to contribute in promoting an alternate worldview to that of consensus reality, namely, a worldview that takes seriously the supernatural.

4. Each denomination can and should *grow in its understanding of conversion, without losing touch with its own distinctives.* Evangelicals thus need to become newly interested in incorporating new believers into programs of spiritual formation (which include a renewed sense of worship) as a necessary part of the evangelistic process. Mainline churches need to move beyond comfortable membership to serious consideration of the faith upon which the church stands and deliberate commitment to that which is distinctive to Christianity. Liturgical churches need to translate the meaning of the liturgy into the life, practice, and beliefs of their members. No one church has a complete understanding when it comes to conversion; each church can learn from the others.

5. *Do not be preoccupied with conversion, but do not neglect it either.* Conversion is only a beginning, merely the first step. It is not the whole of the Christian life. In fact, the proof of conversion is the fruit of one's life. To be preoccupied with conversion only is to neglect what conversion is meant to introduce: life in which there is conscious awareness of God and God's love. To neglect conversion, however, is to forget that all pilgrimages have a beginning; without the beginning, no journey is possible.

It would be ideal if each Christian group could embrace and implement these five points. In the real world, however, change occurs slowly; old animosities die hard, and new ways of viewing the realities closest to us evoke resistance. What might we realistically expect? In the short term our hope might be to influence some within our traditions to broaden their view of conversion (and hence evangelism). For evangelicals to realize that genuine conversion is a process for most people, not an event, is a significant step forward. And for mainline Christians to explore the difference between nominal and vital faith could bring real change. As for liturgical Christians, to see the power of personal experience in the context of sacramental worship would address some of their issues. Beyond that, it would be wonderful if we looked upon one another less as enemies and more as people whose theological commitments are real, deep, and reasoned, even if we disagree with those reasons. Perhaps we could even learn to cooperate in outreach to those without faith traditions who are fascinated by the spiritual and seeking to know God.

Notes

1. Beside works mentioned in the notes below, recently published studies of conversion include Ronald Crandall, *The Contagious Witness: Exploring Christian Conversion* (Nashville: Abingdon Press, 1999); Alan Kreider, *The Change of Conversion and the Origin of Christendom* (Harrisburg, Pa.: Trinity Press, 1999); Richard Fletcher, *The Barbarian Conversion: From Paganism to Christianity* (New York: H. Holt, 1998); Christopher Lamb and M. Darrol Bryant, eds., *Religious Conversion: Contemporary Practices and Controversies* (New York: Cassell Academic, 1999); Lawrence J. Epstein, *Questions and Answers on Conversion to Judaism* (Northvale, N.J.: Jason Aronson, 1998); and Fenggang Yang, *Chinese Christians in America: Conversion, Assimilation, and Adhesive Identities* (University Park: Pennsylvania State Univ. Press, 1999).

2. In his masterful volume *Conversion in the New Testament* (Collegeville, Minn.: Liturgical Press, 1994), Ronald Witherup states: "After careful consideration I have come to believe that the NT shows a fairly uniform teaching about conversion with minimal evidence for a dramatic evolution of the concept" (p. 2).

3. Richard Peace, *Conversion in the New Testament: Paul and the Twelve* (Grand Rapids: Eerdmans, 1999), pp. 17–19.

4. Scot McKnight, *Turning to Jesus: The Sociology of Conversion in the Gospels* (Louisville, Ky.: Westminster John Knox Press, 2002), pp. 1–2.

5. For a discussion and critique of this view of "witnessing," see my article "Holy Conversation: The Lost Art of Witness," *Word and World* 22, no. 3 (Summer 2002): 255–63.

6. In my book I call this approach encounter evangelism. For a critique, see *Conversion in the New Testament*, chap. 11, pp. 285–308.

7. Donald Miller, *Reinventing American Protestantism: Christianity in the New Millennium* (Berkeley: Univ. of California Press, 1997), pp. 171–72.

8. When we were students at Fuller Seminary in the 1960s, my wife and

I helped start the mission organization African Enterprise, which does citywide evangelism in Africa and elsewhere. When we returned from South Africa, we helped start Clear Light Productions, a media-based evangelistic organization located in Boston. I have been a professor of evangelism at evangelical seminaries for over twenty-five years.

9. In *Conversion in the New Testament* I argue for the normalcy of conversion as a process.

10. John Wimber with Kevin Springer, *Power Evangelism*, rev. ed. (San Francisco: HarperSanFrancisco, 1985).

11. McKnight, *Turning to Jesus*, p. 5.

12. Donald McKim, "The Mainline Protestant Understanding of Conversion" in *Handbook of Religious Conversion*, ed. H. Newton Malony and Samuel Southard (Birmingham, Ala.: Religious Education Press, 1992), pp. 130–35.

13. I say this as a United Church of Christ minister and as one whose role as a seminary professor takes him into a number of mainline contexts.

14. G. W. Allport, "The Religious Context of Prejudice," *Journal for the Scientific Study of Religion* 5 (1966), and Allport and J. M. Ross, "Personal Religious Orientation and Prejudice," *Journal of Personality and Social Psychology* 5 (1967): 432–43. See also my discussion of Allport in *Conversion in the New Testament*, pp. 315–16.

15. As in the widespread Alpha movement.

16. McKnight, *Turning to Jesus*, p. 7.

17. Augustine, *Confessions* and *Enchiridion*, trans. and ed. Albert Outler, as found at Ethereal Library (www.ccel.org), book 8, chap. 11. Deal Hudson calls Augustine's *Confessions* "the dominating text of Catholic conversion" and identifies Augustine as the Catholic convert par excellence ("The Catholic View of Conversion," in *Handbook of Religious Conversion*, ed. H. Newton Malony and Samuel Southard [Birmingham, Ala.: Religious Education Press, 1992], p. 109).

18. See Walter Conn, ed., *Christian Conversion: A Developmental Interpretation of Autonomy and Surrender* (Mahwah, N.J.: Paulist Press, 1986); Bernard Lonergan, *Grace and Freedom: Operative Grace in the Thought of St. Thomas Aquinas* (New York: Herder & Herder, 1971); and three books by Donald Gelpi, S.J.: *Charism and Sacrament: A Theology of Christian Conversion* (Mahwah, N.J.: Paulist Press, 1976); *The Conversion Experience: A Reflective Process for RCIA Participants and Others* (Mahwah, N.J.: Paulist Press, 1988); and *Committed Worship: A Sacramental Theology for Converting Christians* (Collegeville, Minn.: Liturgical Press, 1993).

19. Hudson, "Catholic View of Conversion," p. 110.

20. Ibid., p. 115, quoting Rahner.

21. Ritual, though, can lead to genuine inner reality later in life.

22. Alexei D. Krindatch, "Orthodox (Eastern Christian) Churches in the United States at the Beginning of a New Millennium: Questions of Nature, Identity, and Mission," *Journal for the Scientific Study of Religion* 41, no. 3 (September 2002): 533–63.

23. Archbishop Paul of Finland, *The Faith We Hold*, trans. Marita Nykänen and Esther Williams (Crestwood, N.Y.: St. Vladimir's Seminary Press, 1999), p. 40.
24. Archimandrite Kallistos Ware, *The Orthodox Way* (Crestwood, N.Y.: St. Vladimir's Seminary Press, 1986), p. 133. The priest marks the newly baptized with the words "The seal of the gift of the Holy Spirit."
25. Ibid., pp. 144–46.
26. Alexander Schmemann, *For the Life of the World: Sacraments and Orthodoxy* (Crestwood, N.Y.: St. Vladimir's Seminary Press, 1988), p. 33. See also pp. 21, 29, 42–44.
27. In neither of the standard texts by Father Kallistos Ware in which the Orthodox position is explained to outsiders is "conversion" listed in the index, nor is "justification" or "sanctification"—two words that figure large in Protestant texts on this particular topic.
28. See, for example, Ion Bria, ed., *Martyria/Mission: The Witness of the Orthodox Churches Today* (Geneva: World Council of Churches, 1980); Ion Bria, ed., *Go Forth in Peace: Orthodox Perspectives on Mission* (Geneva: World Council of Churches, 1986); James Stamoolis, *Eastern Orthodox Mission Theology Today*, American Society of Missiology Series, no. 10 (Maryknoll, N.Y.: Orbis Books, 1986); George Lemopoulos, ed., *Your Will Be Done: Orthodoxy in Mission* (Geneva: WCC Publications, 1989); Luke Alexander Veronis, *Missionaries, Monks, and Martyrs: Making Disciples of All Nations* (Minneapolis: Light & Life Publishing, 1994). I find it interesting that many of these books on missiology are published by non-Orthodox presses.
29. Stamoolis, *Eastern Orthodox Mission Theology Today*, p. 54. Stamoolis quotes here from N. A. Nissiotis, "The Ecclesiological Foundation of Mission from the Orthodox Point of View," *Greek Orthodox Theological Review* 7 (1961–62): 31.
30. Stamoolis, *Eastern Orthodox Mission Theology Today*, pp. xi–xii.
31. To continue one's conversion process is an idea drawn from Catholic theology, which understands conversion as something that continues throughout our pilgrimage of faith. Indeed, the same dynamic of repentance and faith that characterizes one's conversion to Christ also characterizes the ongoing process of transformation. The issues are different, but the process is the same.
32. Timothy Ware gives a nuanced view of this position: "By God's grace the Orthodox Church possesses the fullness of truth (so its members are bound to believe), but there are other Christian communions which possess to a greater or lesser degree a genuine measure of Orthodoxy. All these facts must be taken into account: one cannot simply say that all non-Orthodox are outside the Church. . . . Such is the view of the more moderate party. But there also exists in the Orthodox Church a more rigorous group, who hold that since Orthodoxy is the Church, anyone who is not Orthodox cannot be a member of the Church" (*The Orthodox Church*, new ed. [Harmondsworth, Middlesex: Penguin Books, 1993], pp. 308–9).

5

Implications of Conversion in the Old Testament and the New

Christopher J. H. Wright

The Hebrew word most commonly associated with repentance and conversion—*sub*—is much more often addressed to Israel than used in connection with the other, noncovenant nations.[1] God most eagerly seeks the conversion of his own people, who seem most often bent on turning away from him in the "conversion" of apostasy rather than turning toward him in the conversion of repentance and restoration. The word *sub* is used of turning in either direction. So any missiological reflection on conversion must wrestle with this issue of the continuous need of God's people for radical conversion themselves, rather than being seen only as the agent of the conversion of others. It is often pointed out that the so-called conversion of Cornelius, for example, was just as much (and necessarily) the conversion of Peter, or the conversion of the Ninevites an (unsuccessful) conversion of Jonah.

In this article we examine what the Bible reveals about those who are converted into allegiance to the God of the Bible and into membership of God's people from a position of having previously stood outside that relationship.[2] What are the implications of such a conversion?

Blessing of the Nations

The familiar words of Genesis 12:3 set the agenda for Israel's missional existence in history. So important are they that Paul calls them the Gospel in advance (Gal. 3:6–8). God declares his intention that through Abraham and his descendants, all nations on earth will be blessed. There is no mention here of this blessing coming by the mechanism of conversion as such. But if the nations are to be blessed, or to find blessing, in the same way as Abraham, then we expect that they must follow the footsteps of his faith in, and obedience to, the God who called him. The path to blessing for Abraham meant leaving his home country (in that sense also turning from his ancestral gods), trusting in the promise of God, walking in obedience, and teaching his household to "keep the way of the LORD by doing righteousness and justice" (Gen. 18:19). Though not described as conversion, some of the key elements are already signaled here: forsaking, trusting, obeying, following.

This hope of blessing for the nations, when it does issue in an offer of, or a call to, conversion, generates some interesting prophetic texts. *Jeremiah* holds out to the nations contemporary with his own the same conditional terms for repentance and restoration that he consistently held out to Judah—at least until Judah had gone beyond the possibility of those options (Jer. 12:14–17). This text is remarkable for the way Jeremiah speaks to the nations words otherwise spoken to his own people. The nations (like Israel) could be uprooted and destroyed, or they could be restored and rebuilt. The deciding factor would be their willingness to (1) identify with and learn the ways of Israel and (2) accept the reality of the living God Yahweh. On those terms they could actually be "established among my people"—a quite remarkable offer, based effectively on conversion. It is difficult for us to grasp this concept of the repentance and conversion of nations (see also 18:1–12), but it stands as an irreducible part of the Old Testament faith.

The Book of *Jonah* stands as the most remarkable illustration of the principles affirmed so starkly in Jeremiah 18. Jonah contains at least two actual conversions (the repentance of the Ninevites and the repentance of Yahweh—his change of plan regarding them) and one conversion stubbornly resisted—that of Jonah himself. If the prophet is intended to represent Israel, then the book is an appeal for their conversion to Yahweh's heartbeat of compassion for the nations.

Isaiah raises the stakes still further. The great vision that he has in common with Micah pictures the nations coming up to Mount Zion in a corporate turning to Yahweh and his ways (Isa. 2:1–5; Mic. 4:1–5). Significantly, the expectation that the nations will eventually do this is taken as motivation for Israel to start doing the same here and now. Isaiah presents this as a challenging call (2:5); Micah states it as a stark contrast between the determination of Israel to walk in the name of Yahweh and the continuing historical fact that the nations walk in the name of their own gods (4:5).

In Isaiah 19, after a scorching declaration of God's judgment on historical Egypt of the prophet's day, the prophet portrays an eschatological future in which the historical relation of Israel and Egypt is turned inside out. "On that day" (the language of the unspecified future), there will be an altar to Yahweh in the midst of Egypt (v. 19)—the land whose

Pharaoh had refused even to acknowledge such a God in his country (Exod. 5:2). Egypt will cry out to Yahweh against their oppressors (as the Hebrews had done against the Egyptians), and he will send them a savior to rescue them (v. 20, a remarkable replay of Moses' mission). Yahweh will strike Egypt with a plague, but this time he will heal them (v. 22). Then comes the key conversion text: "They will return to the Lord, and he will listen to their supplications and heal them" (v. 22). What follows is even more amazing. On the basis of this conversion to Yahweh, Egypt, along with Assyria, will join Israel as part of the people of Yahweh. "On that day Israel will be the third with Egypt and Assyria, a blessing in the midst of the earth, whom the Lord of hosts has blessed, saying, 'Blessed be Egypt my people, and Assyria the work of my hands, and Israel my heritage'" (vv. 24–25).

Not only, then, will these ancient enemies of Israel be the beneficiaries of the Abrahamic covenant (that is, they will receive the explicit blessing of Yahweh), but also they will become the agents of Abraham's blessing—they will share in the task of being "a blessing on the earth." The converted become the converting; the blessed become the blessers.

There is something profound here about the nature of conversion: in conversion people receive the names, the identity, the mission, the privilege, of Israel; yet they preserve the ethnic and cultural identity that is theirs by creation. This combination is not surprising when we remember that the purpose of God's election of Israel was for the restoration of creation. Even before Paul developed his second-Adam Christology, there was a Jewish tradition that regarded Abraham as God's fresh start for humanity—a new Adam. Certainly Paul could affirm that if anybody turns to Christ and is "in him," then that person is not just an heir of Abraham but also a new creation.

Radical Displacement of All Other Gods

From the Old Testament perspective, conversion has three major implications. In the first place, the nations that set foot on the road to Yahweh in Zion will abandon their walking in the name of their own gods (Mic. 4:1–5). The ends of the earth that turn to Yahweh to be saved will accept the demonstrable futility of "a god that cannot save" (Isa. 45:20). Instead, they will universally acknowledge that "only in the Lord" are "righteousness" [probably equivalent to saving righteousness, see v. 21—"a righteous God and a Savior"] and "strength" (v. 24). The conversion of Egypt includes the sole acknowledgment of Yahweh, following the exposure through judgment of the worthlessness of the idols they had previously consulted (Isa. 19:3). The nations that will come to the light that will shine from Israel in Isaiah 60 will "proclaim the praise of the LORD" (v. 6), no longer that of their own gods, and their offerings "shall be acceptable on my altar" (v. 7), not at the shrines of other gods.

This expectation is turned into a missional vision and summons in Psalm 96. A new song is to be sung. This new song remixes the old words, for the content is nothing other than the name, the salvation, the glory, and the marvelous deeds of Yahweh (vv. 1–3). These phrases are culled from the old, old story of Yahweh and his love. Yahweh's name—revealed at the burning bush; Yahweh's salvation—as they marched out of Egypt; Yahweh's glory—in tabernacle and temple; Yahweh's marvelous deeds—the etcetera of the great epic of their national history. These were the lyrics Israel had been singing ever since they crossed the Red Sea. What is new is *where* they are now to be sung, and *who* is going to be singing them—"all the earth . . . among the nations . . . among all the peoples." The new song makes the old words true for new singers. Conversion of the nations thus implies not only the acceptance of Israel's *God*, but also acceptance of the saving significance of Israel's *story*.

The ironic historical background to such a vision was the fact that Israel, who should have been the choirmaster for the singing of this new song among the nations, was instead busy singing the songs of the nations by going after their gods instead of preserving their exclusive, covenantal loyalty to Yahweh. So while the psalmists applied their faith imagination to the conversion of the nations, the prophets had to apply their rhetorical energy to the conversion of Israel.

Ethical Transformation

The nations will come up to Yahweh in Zion with clear ethical intent: conversion will mean a change of "walk." The Lord will "teach us his ways" so that "we may walk in his paths" (Isa. 2:3)—the very thing that Israel also needed to learn. The ways of Yahweh should have been the ways of Israel, and in that ideal sense, the nations who wished to convert and be restored by Yahweh, according to Jeremiah, would need to learn the ways of Israel as well as acknowledging the sole deity of Yahweh (Jer. 12:16). The great challenge presented to apostate Israel by Elijah was that they should turn from worshiping Baal to acknowledge Yahweh alone as God. The narrative makes it clear that this ought to have been more than a change of merely verbal or cultic allegiance. The worship of Baal was what legitimated the actions of Jezebel and Ahab—that is, trampling on justice, judicial murder, and confiscation of land by unfettered royal power. The worship of Yahweh demanded a social ethic of economic justice and limits on political power, which would preserve a land safe for Naboths to live in.

The story of the conversion of Nebuchadnezzar in Daniel 4 involves not only his eventual recognition that "heaven rules" but also his acceptance of Daniel's amazing counsel: "Atone for [or break off] your sins with righteousness, and your iniquities with mercy to the oppressed" (Dan. 4:27). Amos could not have put it better. Conversion entailed moral change in the area of social and political responsibility—even for pagan kings. Conversion, in this case, also included a return to sanity, implying that worship of false gods that permits arrogant imperialism and flagrant exploitation is actually a kind of madness. In both of the above cases, conversion was addressed to the political, social, and economic spheres, not merely to religious allegiance.

In the light of this strongly ethical dimension of conversion, there is even greater significance to the term Jesus chose to use in his so-called Great Commission—namely, to go and *disciple* the nations. For this too is an ethical term, calling for a radical change of personal allegiance and a range of ethical commitments. Sadly, one must admit that much evangelical mission has handled the Great Commission as a mandate only for a rather narrowly defined evangelism, omitting the biblical emphasis on discipleship, teaching, and obedience that these verses contain.

End to Commitment to War

Both Isaiah and Micah in their vision of the conversion of the nations envisage the effect of their submission to the judicial sovereignty of Yahweh. The diversion of so much effort and so many resources, things that could be used productively to nourish human life, into weapons of destruction will cease. Nations will not take up the sword against one another and will not "learn war" any more. The portrayal of war as something that consumes resources, and as an acquired skill that generates its own lethal pedagogy, is frighteningly realistic. Only conversion to the living God and his ways can bring an end to both. Psalm 46, which pictures the present reality of the nations in tumult, ends with the great statement of hope that God "makes wars cease to the end of the earth" and recognizes that this can come about only when the nations acknowledge that Yahweh is God, when he is "exalted among the nations." Conversion of the nations to the living God is the only hope for world peace.

We recognize this as ultimately an eschatological hope. Only God can, and only God will, put an end to war. But the fact that we have this sure hope, like other aspects of biblical eschatology, should fire us to appropriate action in the present that erects a signpost to the future. We live now under the ethical mandate of the beatitude "Blessed are the peacemakers, for they shall be called sons of God"—that is, they will have the character of God by working now for what God will ultimately complete.

Implications for Missions

What is the meaning of the conversion of the nations in the Old Testament for New Testament faith and mission? In what sense, if any, are we to call nations to conversion today? Since the people of God now exist as a multinational community in Christ and cannot be identified with any single nation or state, can we even speak of a "converted nation" or a "Christian nation"? Do we expect nations to display the marks of Christian discipleship, as set out, for example, in the Sermon on the Mount? If not, where do we take this Old Testament theme?

First, there is no hermeneutical validity in seeking to reestablish some kind of political theocracy on Old Testament lines in modern nations. Even in Israel the marriage of faith community and royal political state was never easy, was frequently compromised, and ended in messy divorce. Attempts to create Christian states, from Constantine to Calvin and beyond, have more often than not ended in tears, tyranny, and torturers.

Second, the clearest fulfillment of the Old Testament message regarding the nations appears in the New Testament mission to the nations. The blessing of the nations, interpreted through the missional mandate of Jesus and the centrifugal mission of the church, is not a matter of the conversion of states and governments, even though church history does contain remarkable cases of the conversion of heads of state who in turn provided access and patronage for the evangelistic work of the church. We are to pray for governments. We are to bless the nations. So one way in which the Old Testament vision of the conversion of the nations is to be worked out is through obedience to the Great Commission—namely, discipling (Matt. 28:19–20) and proclaiming repentance and forgiveness (Luke 24:47).

Third, however, we should remember the paradigmatic nature of Israel in the plan of God.[3] They were intended to be a light to the nations. What God did in and for them and what God said and revealed to them were all ultimately aimed at a wider audience—the rest of the nations, for whose blessing Israel was called into existence in the first place. One of the most glaringly obvious messages in the scriptures of Israel is that God holds kings, governments, and nations to account. God, as supreme moral judge of all the earth, demands that they do justice, love mercy, and walk humbly (Mic. 6:8, originally addressed individually but also, given the whole context of the prophets, a message for governments). Therefore it seems entirely right that part of our Christian responsibility, standing as the spiritual heirs of the prophets of Israel, is to call nations and their governments to account and, where necessary, to repentance. Even in praying for them, we are presuming the reality of the higher sovereignty of God, to whom they are responsible. So, like Daniel, we should have the courage to say, even to secular governments, "Break off your sins with righteousness, and your iniquities with mercy to the oppressed" (Dan. 4:27).

Conversion of Individuals in the Old Testament

While the promise of God to Abraham that the nations would be blessed through him points toward an eschatological ingathering that only God would accomplish, the history of Israel in the Old Testament period does testify to significant numbers of those who stood originally outside the covenant community being blessed through it, coming into membership of it, or professing some kind of conversion to Yahweh.[4] This phenomenon is more at the level of individuals or groups, rather than of nations, but it does offer some interesting perspectives on our inquiry.

From the very beginning, Israel emerges into history and onto the pages of the Old Testament as a "mixed multitude." The exodus narrative records that a great many other people left Egypt along with the Israelites (Exod. 12:37–39), and the next section of text outlines some regulations for the Passover to take into account the presence of such foreigners and to give criteria for their acceptability or otherwise at the Passover meal. Later we see that there was a substantial resident alien population at the time of the united monarchy (2 Chron. 2:17–18). Throughout, there was a remarkable openness to the inclusion and absorption of aliens into the Israelite community at various levels—including religious.

The Passover regulations make it clear that a *resident alien* could be included in the worshiping community, celebrating the foundational event in Israel's redemptive history, provided he accepted circumcision (Exod. 12:48–49). On that basis he and his family were to be treated as fully equal to the native born. This religious inclusion of "converted," or assimilated, persons then extended in many directions: the annual feasts (Deut. 16:11, 14), the Day of Atonement (Lev. 16:29), the ceremony of covenant renewal and commitment (Deut. 29:11; 31:12), and inclusion in Sabbath rest (Exod. 20:9–11; 23:12; Deut. 5:12–15). Since many of these events were part of the social and economic rhythm of the life of the community, the inclusion of the converted alien was very comprehensive. Indeed, because of the vulnerable social status of such people, the law repeatedly advocates their protection: from general oppression (Exod. 22:21; Lev. 19:33), from injustice in court (Exod. 23:9; Deut. 10:17–19; 24:17–18), and from exploitation in the workplace (Deut. 24:14–15). In short, they are to be treated as equal before the law with the native born (Lev. 19:34). For the resident alien, then, conversion—at least according to the ideals of Israelite law—meant complete *inclusion, participation, and equality* within the living community of God's people.

The position of the *foreigner* who remained one (i.e., did not assimilate through circumcision) was more ambiguous. But two texts are quite remarkable in their vision for such people. At the dedication of the temple in 1 Kings 8, in the midst of praying that God would hear the prayers of his people Israel in all kinds of circumstances, Solomon prays thus for non-Israelites: "When a foreigner, who is not of your people Israel, comes from a distant land because of your name—for they shall hear of your great name, your mighty hand, and your outstretched arm—when a foreigner comes and prays toward this house, then hear in heaven your dwelling place, and *do according to all that the foreigner calls to you, so that all the peoples of the earth may know your name and fear you*" (vv. 41–43).

This text is remarkable in its very anticipation that such things would happen—that is, that foreigners would be so attracted to the power and presence of this God, Yahweh the God of Israel, that they would come from afar to pray for his blessing. But it is also remarkable in the reason Solomon offers as an incentive to God for answering the foreigner's prayer—namely, that the name of Yahweh should be known universally. We may not know if the text anticipates the *conversion* of the foreigner to become a worshiper of Yahweh (though it may be implied by the very fact that the foreigner brings a request to Yahweh's temple), but the vision is amazingly missional in its scope (and it is repeated at v. 60). For the foreigner, then, clear implications of conversion include, at the very least, gratitude for answered prayer and the spreading fame of the name of Yahweh.

Isaiah 56 also addresses individual foreigners with words of hope.

From having been previously excluded from Yahweh's sacred assembly,[5] they are promised "the full works," as conversion experiences go: they can come to the holy hill; they can come into Yahweh's house; they can even bring their sacrifices to the altar (vv. 6–7). Those who come from the unclean world of the foreign nations are accepted at the holy altar of Yahweh. On what basis was this inclusion and acceptance offered? Their wholehearted commitment to the Lord, in covenant service, love, worship, and obedience (v. 6). The *conversion* is very clear; their *inclusion* is equally emphatic. Notably, the words of inclusion are spoken directly by God; the assumption is that the existing covenant community should echo the welcome.

The classic Old Testament convert is Ruth. Indeed, one might say that the book affords us one of the most beautiful descriptions of conversion, when Boaz sums up what Ruth has done: "May the LORD reward you for your deeds, and may you have a full reward from the LORD, the God of Israel, under whose wings you have come for refuge!" (Ruth 2:12).[6] For Ruth, the result of conversion was her experience of the matching *hesed* (i.e., faithful, loyal love) of Boaz. The model response of Boaz to this vulnerable "convert" provided for her, protected her, and eventually incorporated her into an Israelite family, in Israel's land, blessed by Israel's God. For Ruth, conversion led to inclusion, not only in the covenant community, but also in the ancestry of the royal house of David and the messianic lineage of Jesus (Matt. 1:5). If Israel was supposed in some way to emulate Boaz (who is certainly presented as a model Israelite), then the book challenges any kind of ethnic exclusivism and calls for a welcoming inclusion of those who make genuine confession of conversion to the Lord God of Israel.

Summing up this section, then, we can immediately see some aspects in common with those noted above with reference to the nations. There is the radical *rejection of other gods* and exclusive commitment to Yahweh. There is *inclusion* within the worshiping community—by the covenant ritual of circumcision (the alien), and by explicit and frequent listing with the rest of the nation in the festivals, covenant ceremonies, and so forth. And there is also the demand for *ethical transformation*: by the foreigner convert's accepting commitment to observe God's covenant law. The conditions for the foreigner are no different from those demanded of apostate Israelites who are called to repent and convert back to true allegiance to Yahweh—let it be in truth and justice (Jer. 4:1–2), and let it involve the radical rejection of oppressive ways and commitment to social compassion, integrity, and honesty (Ezek. 33:14–16).

New Testament Perspectives on Conversion

As in the Old Testament, so in the Gospels the call to repent and "convert" is addressed primarily to Israel. God's people need to return to their God. But our theme asks us to look rather at the conversion of those who, from outside the believing community, "turned to the Lord." This focus sends us primarily to the Book of Acts, though obviously Paul addresses the issue also in some of his letters. It seems that the same necessities of conversion are found in the New Testament as in the Old Testament, and the same expectations of what ought to follow for the convert.

Thus, first, there is the clear demand for *the radical rejection and displacement of all other gods* than the living God, now revealed through his Son Jesus Christ. Paul makes this point in some haste and embarrassment in Lystra (Acts 14:15–17). He repeats it as the burden of his missionary career since his own "conversion"[7] (Acts 26:18). And in case it might be thought that this represents the Gentile Luke's slanted reporting on the matter, Paul himself expresses it in virtually identical terms in what may be his earliest letter: "You turned to God from idols, to serve a living and true God, and to wait for his Son from heaven, whom he raised from the dead—Jesus" (1 Thess. 1:9).

Second, *conversion leads to inclusion.* This can be risky. We are well aware of the danger often faced by converts: danger from the communities they have left and are thought to have betrayed. Certainly Paul experienced such hostility repeatedly. But those who have the courage to welcome the convert also take risks of misunderstanding from both sides. Ananias certainly needed courage and faith to welcome Saul of Tarsus as a brother within hours of his conversion (Acts 9:10–19). Alleged converts can be false, intent on subverting the faithful from within. The fear of Saul by the vulnerable church in Jerusalem could have barred him from inclusion and welcome. But the risky friendship of Barnabas at that crucial time achieved it.

But there is also theological risk. And sometimes only God can persuade people to take that risk—even if he has to use angels, visions, and ultimately a whole church council. Thus, Peter's acceptance of Cornelius into baptized membership of the new followers of the Way, because of his manifest faith in the message of Christ and the evident work of the Holy Spirit, exposed Peter to severe criticism from fellow Jewish believers. Peter's explanation was initially accepted, to general rejoicing (Acts 11:18). The issue rumbled on, however, and was brought to a head by the success of Paul's mission among the Gentiles. Should these converts to Christ be accepted and included without also becoming proselytes to Judaism? What should be required of them? Such questions about the implications of conversion were exactly what the church faced as a result of the success of its own mission (Acts 15:5).[8] The Council of Jerusalem in Acts 15 addressed two issues—the *theological grounds* of inclusion, and the *practical follow-up* to inclusion for those who had professed conversion. The theology was sorted out on the basis of Old Testament scriptures. The ingathering of the Gentiles, far from being a problem in relation to the scriptures, is precisely their fulfillment. (James quotes Amos 9:11–12; he could have quoted at least a dozen other texts of similar import.) The practical problem is sorted out with a wonderfully inclusive pragmatism: "It is my judgment, therefore, that *we should not make it difficult* for the Gentiles who are turning to God" (Acts 15:19 NIV). Would that this principle operated in all evangelistic and discipleship programs!

Paul's letters affirm very strongly this new inclusion of his converts in the community of this new people of God. Ephesians 2:11–22 is probably the locus classicus, with Paul telling his Gentile readers that from being far off, they have been brought near. From being aliens and strangers (to Israel's citizenship, Israel's promises, Israel's hope, Israel's God, and Israel's Messiah), they have now become citizens of God's own country, members of God's own family, and the place of God's own dwelling—a radical conversion indeed! And it has been argued that a major purpose of all Paul's letters, indirectly, is to foster this sense of new identity and inclusion among his convert communities. They must know who they now are because of their allegiance to Christ.

Third and finally, it is clear, also from Paul's letters, that conversion also involved *radical ethical transformation*. Paul's account to Festus of his ministry includes so much of importance. Not only was Paul intent on *turning* people from the worship of idols to the living God, not only did he offer such converts the *inclusion* of having "a place among those who are sanctified" (Acts 26:18), he also "preached that they should repent and turn to God and *do deeds consistent with repentance*" (v. 20). Very John the Baptist, very Jesus, very James, very Jeremiah.

Notes

1. The equivalent word in the New Testament, *epistrepho*, is more commonly used of the conversion of unbelievers.
2. The approach adopted will be fairly synchronic; that is, I will not be concerned to trace historical developments within the literature and traditions of the Bible or to take into account other critical issues of that nature.

3. I have explained what I understand by the paradigmatic nature of Israel much more fully in my book *Living as the People of God: The Relevance of Old Testament Ethics* (U.S. title: *An Eye for an Eye*) (Leicester and Downers Grove, Ill.: InterVarsity Press, 1983). A fully revised and updated edition is forthcoming.

4. Charles Scobie makes much of this distinction in his discussion of the theme of the nations in biblical theology: he speaks of eschatological ingathering of the nations (an act of God, which the New Testament sees as initiated in the Gentile mission) and historical incorporation (the choice of individuals or groups in Old Testament times). C. H. H. Scobie, "Israel and the Nations: An Essay in Biblical Theology," *Tyndale Bulletin* 43, no. 2 (1992): 283–305.

5. The laws of Deuteronomy 23:1–8 are thought by some scholars to be the background to Isaiah 56, though it is a debatable point.

6. Note, in view of comments below, that it was to Yahweh that Ruth had fled, not primarily to Israel (except of course geographically). Throughout the narrative she continues to be called "the Moabite."

7. I acknowledge that some prefer not to use the term "conversion" of Paul's Damascus road experience, since he was obviously not a pagan converting to the God of Israel, nor a Jew converting to Christianity in an anachronistic sense. Nevertheless, Paul's encounter with Christ included a repentance, a turning, an acknowledgment of the lordship of the risen Christ, and a commissioning—all of which may be fairly described as conversion, even if the term needs to be carefully qualified in the case of Jews who, like Paul, find in Jesus of Nazareth a fulfillment of their ancestral faith.

8. The answer clearly was that they should be converts to Christ, not proselytes to Judaism. This conclusion, in Andrew Walls's analysis, was an utterly key decision and distinction at this early stage of the church. It enabled a genuine Greek church to emerge. To become a Christian meant converting to Christ—that is, turning everything in one's life, history, and culture toward Christ for redemptive purging and re-creation. It did not mean becoming ethnically or culturally a "proselyte"—a naturalized Jew—for that route preserved the old ethnic distinction between Jew and Gentile, which, as the very heartbeat of Paul's gospel passionately affirmed, had been utterly dissolved by the cross of Christ. As Walls commented (in conversation), Paul seems not to have got so angry with the Corinthians, who at least were attempting to be genuinely Greek Christians, even if they were making a mess of it, as he did with the Galatians, who were denying the universality of the Gospel by reasserting an ethnic, national, law-based foundation for belonging to God's people. The vast, global, and cultural diversity of the Christian church today is the legitimate fruit of this essential distinction between conversion (i.e., conversion to *Christ* within any culture) and proselytism (which essentially says, "You first must *become like us*"). Sadly, Christian mission has not always preserved this distinction.

6

Reading the Bible in the Global South

Philip Jenkins

In recent years, Christian denominations worldwide have been deeply divided over issues of gender, sexual morality, and homosexuality, and gatherings of the worldwide Anglican Communion have been particularly contentious. On one occasion, two bishops were participating in a Bible study, one an African Anglican, the other a U.S. Episcopalian. As the hours went by, tempers frayed as the African expressed his confidence in the clear words of Scripture, while the American stressed the need to interpret the Bible in the light of contemporary scholarship. Eventually, the African bishop asked in exasperation, "If you don't *believe* the Scripture, why did you bring it to us in the first place?" As worldwide Anglican tensions have escalated since 2003, attitudes to biblical authority have proved increasingly divisive. Kenyan archbishop Benjamin Nzimbi has even declared, "Our understanding of the Bible is different from theirs. We are two different churches."

Though Anglicanism is an important tradition, claiming some 80 million adherents worldwide, it accounts for only 4 percent of all Christians. The kind of split that we have seen in the Anglican Church has emerged across denominations, especially in matters of gender and sexuality. Other churches have watched Anglican conflicts with some alarm, fearing that perhaps they might be getting a foretaste of future debates among Lutherans, Methodists, Presbyterians, and, perhaps someday, even Roman Catholics. Similar disputes surface not just in international meetings but also in North American religious communities with large immigrant populations.

North vs. South

The divisions churches have experienced tend to fall along lines of what has come to be referred to as North and South, with Christians in the generally richer northern countries favoring a liberal interpretation of Scripture, and those in the generally poorer South maintaining a more conservative Christianity and traditional view of Scripture. We often encounter conservative themes in the religious thought of African and Asian Christians, specifically in their attitudes toward the Bible. They often include a much greater respect for the authority of Scripture, especially in matters of morality; a willingness to accept the Bible as an inspired text and a tendency to literalism; a special interest in supernatural elements of Scripture, such as miracles, visions, and healings; a belief in the continuing power of prophecy; and a veneration for the Old Testament, which is treated as equally authoritative as the New. Biblical traditionalism and literalism are still more marked in the independent churches and in denominations rooted in the Pentecostal tradition, but similar currents are also found among Roman Catholics. Even a cursory acquaintance with African or Asian Christianity reveals the pervasive importance it gives to the Bible and biblical stories.

I am not proposing a simple kind of geographic determinism that shapes religious belief. We can hardly speak of how all Africans approach a given topic, any more than we can speak for all Europeans on a given point: Scots may think one thing, Sicilians quite another. Nor are these societies themselves in any sense uniform: Scots laborers presumably read one way, Scots professors another. Attitudes toward biblical interpretation and authority follow no neat North-South pattern. We find "Southern" expressions in the North in the form of charismatic, fundamentalist, and deeply traditionalist belief, while liberals and "Northern"-style feminists are by no means unknown in even the most fervently traditional-minded African and Asian churches. Also, despite all the financial difficulties faced particularly by African universities, global South scholars form a distinguished part of the global community of biblical learning. They read and publish in the mainstream journals of Europe and North America and reinforce international ties at conferences and seminars. Naturally enough, given the colonial and postcolonial histories of their nations, many such scholars have been shaped by radical theological perspectives, and by liberationist and feminist thought.[1]

Global South churches produce a spectrum of theologies and interpretations, just as churches in the United States do. The North-South difference is rather one of emphasis. Though conservative and literalist approaches are widely known in the global North (which mainstream political discourse and the media are fond of labeling as controversial and reactionary), in the South biblical and theological conservatism clearly represents the Christian mainstream.

Several factors contribute to the global South's more literal interpretation of Scripture. For one thing, the Bible has found a congenial home among communities who identify with the social and economic realities it portrays, no less than the political environments in which Christians find themselves. For the growing churches of the global South, the Bible speaks to everyday real-world issues of poverty and debt, famine and urban crisis, racial and gender oppression, and state brutality and persecution. The omnipresence of poverty in these societies promotes awareness of the transience of life, of the dependence of individuals and nations on God, and of the untrustworthiness of the secular order.

For another, Christianity, like any dynamic ideological or religious system, adapts to respond to its rivals or neighbors. Joel Carpenter notes how Euro-American academic theology, facing the challenges of secularism, postmodernity, and changing concepts of gender, still focuses on "European thinkers and post-Enlightenment intellectual issues. Western theologians, liberal and conservative, have been addressing the faith to an age of doubt and secularity, and to the competing salvific claims of secular ideologies." Global South Christians, in contrast, do not live in an age of doubt but must instead deal with competing claims to faith. Their views are shaped by interaction with their different neighbors and the very different issues they raise, whether Muslims, traditional religionists in Africa and Asia, or members of the great Asian religions. Accordingly, "the new Christianity will push theologians to address the faith to poverty and social injustice; to political violence, corruption, and the meltdown of law and order; and to Christianity's witness amidst religious plurality. They will be dealing with the need of Christian communities to make sense of God's self-revelation to their pre-Christian ancestors."[2] In all these matters, they find abundant material in the Scriptures, often in passages that mean little to Northern-world theologians.

In consequence, the "Southern" Bible carries a freshness and authenticity that adds vastly to its credibility as an authoritative source and as a guide for daily living. In this context, it is difficult to make the familiar Euro-American argument that the Bible was written for a totally alien society with which moderns can scarcely identify, so that its detailed moral laws cannot be applied in the contemporary world. Cultures that readily identify with biblical worldviews find it easier to read the Bible not just as historical fact but also as relevant instruction for daily conduct.

Old Testament

The Southern sense of identification with the Bible is especially strong for the Old Testament. Cultural affinities with the biblical world lead

African and Asian Christians to a deep affection for the Old Testament as *their* story, *their* book. In Africa particularly, Christians have long been excited by the obvious cultural parallels that exist between their own societies and those of the Hebrew Bible, especially in the world of the patriarchs. While the vast majority of modern Africans have no direct experience of nomadism or polygamy, they can at least relate to the kind of society in which such practices were commonplace.[3]

Equally familiar in these societies is the very prominent element of sacrifice, such as existed in Hebrew ritual. In much of Africa, social events still frequently involve some kind of sacrifice or libation, as do celebrations of key events in the ceremonial year. In a much-quoted study, Justin Ukpong has drawn many parallels between the Hebrew practice of sacrifice as described in Leviticus and the modern institution as known among the Ibibio people of southeastern Nigeria.[4] Another observer's account of a modern African society also reveals striking similarities with the Old Testament mind-set: "In a Nigerian traditional setting, salvation is seen as a group affair and it is in the present. For a community to be saved from some kind of epidemic, afflictions, abominations, bad death and even wars, a price is paid. There is an atonement to please the gods. The medium of atonement is the shedding of the blood of animals."[5]

African and Asian readers need no gloss to understand Hebrew customs and forms that strike North Americans as archaic and incomprehensible. Why was God angry with David for taking a census of the people of Israel? Gikuyu readers in Kenya instantly appreciate the taboos associated with counting and enumeration.[6] Unlike their Western counterparts, moreover, many African and Asian Christians think it only reasonable that the Bible should include lengthy genealogies for key figures, most obviously for Jesus himself: how else does one situate a figure and assert the basis on which he claims authority? Without roots and family, a political or religious leader has no plausible claim to one's loyalty or even attention. Chinese scholar Fook-Kong Wong notes that "the genealogical lists in Chronicles bear witness to God's intimate knowledge and remembrance of his people."[7]

For African believers, the pleasant shock of recognition is especially strong in the first twelve or so chapters of Genesis. In the calling of Abram, readers with any sense of African roots will encounter many well-known ideas. The story tells of the origin of a tribe or clan with particular claims to a precious tract of land and of a promise sealed by the construction of an altar and an act of sacrifice, and it emphasizes the rights of a community rather than those of an individual or a nuclear family. The story even takes place near a sacred tree. And the movements of the patriarchal clans are often driven by the endemic threat of famine, a threat easily understood in Africa today. In his analysis of the first eleven chapters of Genesis, a study that has had a profound influence on African Bible scholarship, Yoruba scholar Modupe Oduyoye comments that "one might call [these chapters] the Scriptures to all human beings, since there is little specifically Jewish in the material, and yet a lot that is Afro-Asiatic."[8]

Andrew Walls once commented, "You do not have to interpret Old Testament Christianity to Africans; they live in an Old Testament world."[9] The seeming Africanness of the patriarchal world helps explain the power of the stunning Malian film *Genesis* (1999), a retelling of the biblical tale of Jacob and Esau in which the hunters and the shepherds appear in thoroughly West African guise. And although today nomadism is becoming an increasingly marginal part of African life, the concept still provides a valuable rhetorical tool in discussions of social and economic conflict. The conflict between nomads and agriculturalists, Cain and Abel, can also symbolize the tensions between country dwellers and city dwellers, colonized and settlers, blacks and whites.[10]

Nor is the affinity between Southern societies and the Old Testament confined to Genesis. Commenting on 1 Samuel, Gerald West lists some thirty "African resonances," ways in which the text rings true to southern African readers today. He includes the dynamics of polygamous families, "endemic conflict with neighboring tribes . . . the need to visit a seer on occasions . . . possession by spirits . . . [and] women dancing and singing in recognition of the exploits of their men." In the Old Testament world as in Africa, men aspired to be "buried with their fathers."[11] South African theologian Madipoane Masenya goes so far as to suggest that there must be something culturally amiss with an African who does not recognize a kinship with the Old Testament.[12] Could an equivalent remark conceivably be made of European or North American Christians today?

Poor and Rich

The southward movement of Christianity involves not only a change in the ethnic composition of the world's believers but also a fundamental shift in their social and economic background. The average Christian in the world today is a poor person, very poor indeed by the standards of the white worlds of North America or western Europe. Also different is the social and political status of African and Asian

Christians, who often represent minorities in countries dominated by other religions or secular ideologies. This historic social change cannot fail to affect attitudes toward the Bible. For many Americans and Europeans, the societies in the Bible—in both Testaments—are distant not only in terms of time and place but also in their everyday assumptions, which are all but incomprehensible. It is easy, then, to argue that the religious and moral ideas that grew up in such an alien setting can have little application for a modern community. Yet exactly the same issues that make the Bible a distant historical record for many Americans and Europeans keep it a living text for the churches of the global South. Musimbi Kanyoro has insightfully remarked, "Those cultures which are far removed from biblical culture risk reading the Bible as fiction."

For many readers in the global South, the Bible is congenial because the world it describes is marked by such currently pressing social problems as famine and plague, poverty and exile, clientelism and corruption. A largely poor readership can readily identify with the New Testament society of peasants and small craftsmen dominated by powerful landlords, imperial forces, and networks of debt and credit. In such a context, the excruciating poverty of Lazarus eating the crumbs beneath the rich man's table is not just an archaeological curiosity but a modern reality both for modern dwellers in villages or small towns and for urban populations, who are often not far removed from their rural roots. And while some resemblances between biblical and modern life might be superficial, their accumulated weight adds greatly to the credibility of the text, to the sense that it is written for a contemporary world. Also, the Bible is seen as providing immediate and often material answers to life's problems.

Particularly appealing to these Southern societies are the parables, in which Jesus incorporated so many observations of contemporary conditions. Writing of contemporary Central America, Francisco Goldman remarks that "Guatemala certainly feels biblical. Sheep, swine, donkeys, serpents—these are everywhere, as are centurions, all manner of wandering false prophets, pharisees, lepers and whores. The poor, rural, mainly Mayan landscape has an aura of the miraculous . . . it is the perfect backdrop for religious parables about fields both barren and fertile, fruits and harvests, hunger and plenty."[13] Across Africa and Asia, millions of modern readers know roads where a traveler is likely to be robbed and left for dead, without much hope of intervention by official agencies. They relate to accounts of streets teeming with the sick. They understand that a poor woman who loses a tiny sum of money would search frantically for coins that could allow her children to eat that night. In many countries, readers appreciate the picture of the capricious rich man who offers hospitality on one occasion but on another demands payment of exorbitant debts and obligations, and who must not on any account be offended. Today, though, the rich person would not be a generic magnate or Hellenistic princeling but a corrupt official of a ruling party.[14]

Jesus lived in an agricultural society intimately familiar with planting and harvest—a world of grain, grapes, and olives—and metaphors from this life pervade his teaching. Many of these metaphors are almost incomprehensible to many modern readers in the global North. Without a commentary, or at least a lively interest in gardening, how many American Christians can make much sense of the critical vine-and-branch metaphor in John 15? And for all the enthusiastic language of "harvest" used by Euro-American evangelicals, few have much idea when the actual physical harvest occurs in their part of the world, and few could say whether last year's harvest was particularly rich or poor. Metaphor apart, how many have actually labored in a real vineyard? Yet most Southern Christians are only a generation or two removed from an agricultural society in which traditional rituals were believed to maintain prosperity. In such a world, the notion of death being required to produce life has an intuitive plausibility that is largely lost in urban societies.

On occasion, the social background of global South readers allows them to see dimensions of the text that have been largely lost in the postindustrial world. I was once talking with some West Africans about the Bible passages that make particularly good sense in an agricultural society. Not surprisingly, they mentioned the parable of the sower and the grain of wheat, but they were also moved by the verse about sowing in sorrow and reaping in joy, from Psalm 126. In the King James version this passage reads as follows: "They that sow in tears shall reap in joy. He that goeth forth and weepeth, bearing precious seed, shall doubtless come again with rejoicing, bringing his sheaves with him" (vv. 5–6). For modern Christians around the world, these verses relate naturally to the resurrection, and to passages like Paul's discussion of the body sown in corruption in 1 Corinthians 15. But why are the sowers weeping in the first place? My friends, though, understood the reality of the situation. When the psalm was composed, they realized, times must have been very hard, and food short, a situation they could identify with. People would have been desperately tempted to eat their seed-corn, but they resisted the temptation because they knew that if they did, they would have nothing to eat the following year. Not only does this setting explain the verse, but the association of sowing and sorrow helps explain the very widespread mourning rituals that in the Middle East and elsewhere accompany sowing, commonly invoking some dying deity.

Wisdom Literature

In addition to these social similarities, global South societies are familiar with the dangers and disasters that faced the biblical world, which seem all but irrelevant in North America today. In such a setting, whole genres in the Bible come alive. It is certainly true of the Wisdom books, including Wisdom-type passages of books like James, which are so easily applied to a world of disaster. Indeed, the appeal of Wisdom stretches across faith traditions. Even the Dalai Lama has praised James highly, especially the declaration that "your life is a vapor," which "beautifully captured" the basic and seemingly universal doctrine of transience.[15] Consider, for example, the Philippines, which, like many other Third World countries, "has seen too many funerals, too many deaths of various causes. None of our days pass without some news of massacre somewhere, death toll at a landslide accident, huge earthquakes claiming hundreds of lives, volcanic eruption tearing down houses and burying entire communities."[16] In 2004 the Western media devoted much attention to the cataclysmic tsunami that killed some 200,000 around the Indian Ocean, but most natural disasters in Asia or Africa receive scant notice.

The Bible's Wisdom literature is so popular in these societies, at least in part because of their profound sense of the transience of life. Of the many beloved passages in the Epistle of James, the one most frequently used for African sermon texts is James 4:14, which seems uncannily relevant to the conditions of everyday life: "Ye know not what shall be on the morrow. For what is your life? It is even a vapor [NIV: a mist], that appeareth for a little time, and then vanisheth away" (KJV). Echoes of this text often resurface in paraphrased form. In the Sudan, which for some forty years has suffered from civil wars and vicious persecution of non-Muslims, one Christian chorus teaches the grim truth, "You are here today but tomorrow you'll be here no more / Our only hope is Jesus Christ, so receive him now."[17] In the aftermath of the 2004 tsunami, sermons in the churches of South and East Asia made great use of James.

This sense of transience and frailty extends not just to individuals and families but also to whole nations. While global North nations certainly experience disasters, very rarely do they threaten the existence of a society or of large numbers of its people. In 2001 shocking terrorism in the United States killed 3,000 people, and the AIDS epidemic has caused hundreds of thousands of deaths since the early 1980s. In 2005, a hurricane all but destroyed a great American city. At no point, however, did such calamities threaten the functioning of the nation. Elsewhere in the world, though, epidemic diseases and natural disasters remain a common part of life, giving a special relevance to the biblical language of plague, drought, and famine.[18]

Under such challenges, nations can literally collapse, a truly frightening idea in a world in which nationality determines so much of our identity. Nations disintegrate as poverty, hunger, and disagreements over natural resources fuel ethnic and political tensions. The failed states that result are the nightmares of international policymakers, as has been the case with Afghanistan, Somalia, Liberia, and Sierra Leone. And in the immense lands of the Congo, war alone has killed some 4 million people over the past decade.[19]

A postcolonial world appreciates the provisional character of nationhood. Realistically or not, Americans, the British, and the French tend to believe that their nations have always existed and will continue to do so, whatever disasters they might experience. In contrast, many African and Asian countries have existed in their present form only for a few decades, often having emerged from long periods of colonization or foreign dominance. With this background, it is easy for them to understand the Old Testament idea that a nation's existence depends upon God's favor. Southern-world Christians identify with Old Testament warnings that righteousness must prevail at the national and communal levels, that the survival of nations is in the hands of a closely observing God, who uses worldly instruments to reward or punish his peoples. When no earthly authority has a plausible claim on our faith, how natural it seems to assert only the absolute truth of the divine as the standard besides which all earthly powers so conspicuously fall short. This approach gives a contemporary feel to the Hebrew prophets, who warned the nation of Israel of the doom that awaited it if it forsook the God who had made the people his own.

Lamentation

The same circumstances of the global South that make Wisdom literature come alive also increase the relevance of the genre of lamentation. Writing against the background of political and religious repression in China, Archie Chi Chung Lee has protested "the loss of lament." Lamentation was in antiquity a well-known genre, a literature of mourning and grief, bemoaning the fall of a state or society, which was also a mainstay of traditional Chinese culture. In the Bible this genre is represented by the Lamentations of Jeremiah. Lee notes that in the West, however, lament no longer maintains its ancient centrality, and he pleads for a reversal of this contemporary ignorance. "The voice of the exiled and desperate community must be released in this current time of sorrow and loss so that grief-stricken and wretched people can make their own voices heard with all their power. . . . For them, the book of Lamentations has survived and, in its role as literature of survival, will continue to provide the means of survival for suffering humanity."[20] A Catholic Bible commentary writes that "Lamentations can be considered as a prayer book for Africans"—a grim statement, but undeniably true.[21]

The prevalence of hunger and natural disaster also helps explain the enormous popularity in Christian Africa and Asia of the Book of Ruth, a tale of a society devastated by famine in which women survive by depending on each other and on trusted kin. In the American context, the book attracts some interest from feminist scholars, and Ruth's plea to Naomi "Entreat me not to leave thee" (1:16) is included in blessing rites for same-sex couples.[22] In the global South, however, the book's interest lies in how the various characters faithfully fulfill their obligations to each other and their relatives. The book becomes a model, even a manual, for a situation that could arise all too easily. Musimbi Kanyoro writes that "the book of Ruth is loved because it has something for everyone in Africa. Africans read this book in a context in which famine, refugee status, tribal or ethnic loyalties, levirate marriages and polygamy are not ancient biblical practices but the normal realities of today."[23] What the North reads in moral or individualistic terms remains for the South social and communal.[24]

In many other ways, too, African and Asian readers can identify strongly with sections of the Bible that mean little to Northern-world believers. I think of passages about healing and spiritual warfare, or of readings that demonstrate a real suspicion of the secular state, particularly in the apocalyptic tradition. But these passages only reinforce the point made here, that the Bible rings so true for African and Asian Christians because it speaks to their daily realities. These Christians can easily echo the eerie words of Martin Luther about the emotional appeal of the text, which underlies the intellectual appeal: "The Bible is alive—it has hands and grabs hold of me, it has feet and runs after me!" Perhaps in the coming decades the Christian world will increasingly be divided by a common Scripture.

Notes

1. Contemporary Bible scholarship from the global South is amply represented, for instance, in R. S. Sugirtharajah, ed., *Voices from the Margin* (Maryknoll, N.Y.: Orbis Books, 1995); Kwok Pui-Lan, *Discovering the Bible in the Non-biblical World* (Maryknoll, N.Y.: Orbis Books, 1995); Daniel Carro and Richard F. Wilson, eds., *Contemporary Gospel Accents* (Macon, Ga.: Mercer Univ. Press, 1996); Gerald O. West and Musa W. Dube, ed., *The Bible in Africa* (Leiden: Brill, 2000); Fernando F. Segovia, *Decolonizing Biblical Studies* (Maryknoll, N.Y.: Orbis Books, 2000); Justin S. Ukpong, Musa W. Dube, Gerald O. West, Alpheus Masoga, Norman K. Gottwald, Jeremy Punt, Tinyiko S. Maluleke, and Vincent L. Wimbush, eds., *Reading the Bible in the Global Village* (Atlanta: Society of Biblical Literature, 2002); John Parratt, ed., *Introduction to Third World Theologies* (Cambridge: Cambridge Univ. Press, 2004); J. N. K. Mugambi and Johannes A. Smit, eds., *Text and Context in New Testament Hermeneutics* (Nairobi: Acton, 2004); Stephen D. Moore and Fernando F. Segovia, *Postcolonial Biblical Criticism* (Edinburgh: T. & T. Clark International, 2005).

2. Joel A. Carpenter, "The Christian Scholar in an Age of Global Christianity" (2004), at http://www.calvin.edu/minds/vol01/issue02/global-christianity.php.

3. See Rebecca Yawa Ganusah, "Pouring Libation to Spirit Powers Among the Ewe-Dome of Ghana," in *The Bible in Africa*, ed. West and Dube, pp. 278–91; Kwesi A. Dickson, *Theology in Africa* (Maryknoll, N.Y.: Orbis Books, 1984); Musimbi R. A. Kanyoro, "Interpreting Old Testament Polygamy Through African Eyes," in *The Will to Arise*, ed. Mercy Amba Oduyoye and Musimbi R. A. Kanyoro (Maryknoll, N.Y.: Orbis Books, 1992), pp. 87–100.

4. Justin S. Ukpong, "Ibibio Sacrifices and Levitical Sacrifices" (Ph.D. diss., Pontifical Univ., Rome, 1990).

5. M. A. Ameagodosu, "Paul's Theology of Salvation in Romans," *Asia Journal of Theology* 23, no. 1 (2000): 44.

6. Sammy Githuku, "Taboos on Counting," in *Interpreting the Old Testament in Africa*, ed. Mary N. Getui, Knut Holter, and Victor Zinkuratire (New York: Peter Lang, 2001), pp. 113–17.

7. Fook-Kong Wong, "1 and 2 Chronicles," in *Global Bible Commentary*, ed. Daniel Patte (Nashville: Abingdon Press, 2004), p. 122.

8. Modupe Oduyoye, *The Sons of the Gods and the Daughters of Men* (Maryknoll, N.Y.: Orbis Books, 1984), p. 11.

9. See http://www.dacb.org/stories/egypt/desert_people.html.

10. Mark McEntire, "Cain and Abel in Africa," in *The Bible in Africa*, ed. West and Dube, pp. 248–59.

11. Gerald West, "1 and 2 Samuel," in *Global Bible Commentary*, ed. Patte, p. 94.

12. Madipoane Masenya, "Wisdom and Wisdom Converge," in *Interpreting the Old Testament in Africa*, ed. Getui et al., p. 145.

13. Francisco Goldman, "Matthew," in *Revelations: Personal Responses to the Books of the Bible*, ed. Richard Holloway (London: Canongate, 2005), p. 210.

14. See Justin S. Ukpong, ed., *Gospel Parables in African Context* (Port Harcourt, Nigeria: Catholic Institute of West Africa Press, 1988).

15. Dalai Lama, "Introduction," in *Revelations*, ed. Holloway, pp. 359–66.

16. Oscar S. Suarez, "That They May Have Life," *CTC Bulletin* 12, no. 2 (1994), at http://www.cca.org.hk/resources/ctc/ctc94-02/9.oscar.htm.

17. Marc Nikkel, "Death Has Come to Reveal the Faith," in *Anglicanism: A Global Communion*, ed. Andrew Wingate, Kevin Ward, Carrie Pemberton, and Wilson Sitshebo (New York: Church Publishing, 1998), p. 74.

18. See for instance "Plague of Locusts Hits Africa," http://www.news24.com/News24/Africa/News/0,6119,2-11-1447_1638319,00.html.

19. Stephen Ellis, *The Mask of Anarchy: The Destruction of Liberia and the Religious Dimension of an African Civil War* (New York: New York Univ. Press, 1999); Roy M. Woodbridge, *The Next World War: Tribes, Cities, Nations, and Ecological Decline* (Toronto: Univ. of Toronto Press, 2004).

20. Archie Chi Chung Lee, "Lamentations," in *Global Bible Commentary*, ed. Patte, pp. 232–33.

21. *The African Bible* (Nairobi: Paulines Publications, 1999), p. 1398.

22. For gay uses of Ruth 1:16, see for instance http://www.mcchurch.org/AM/Template.cfm?Section=Search&Template=/Search/SearchDisplay.cfm. Click on "Our Story Too Part 2." See also http://www.buddybuddy.com/vows-3.html.

23. Musimbi Kanyoro, "Reading the Bible from an African Perspective," *Ecumenical Review* 51, no. 1 (1999): 18–24.

24. Wong Wai Ching Angela, "Building Communities," *CTC Bulletin* 20, no. 1 (2004), at http://www.cca.org.hk/resources/ctc/ctc04-01/ctc04-01b.htm; Viola Raheb, "Women in Contemporary Palestinian Society: A Contextual Reading of the Book of Ruth," in *Feminist Interpretation of the Bible and the Hermeneutics of Liberation*, ed. Silvia Schroer and Sophia Bietenhard (New York: Continuum, 2003), pp. 88–93.

7

The Challenge of Churchless Christianity: An Evangelical Assessment

Timothy C. Tennent

The explosive growth of the church in the non-Western world is raising many new questions regarding the doctrine of the church. In his book *The Next Christendom: The Coming of Global Christianity*,[1] Philip Jenkins has highlighted the vigorous growth of Christianity in the non-Western world. Jenkins predicts that if current trends continue, six countries in the world will have 100 million Christians by the year 2050, but only one of the six (the United States) will be located in the industrialized West.[2] Within the next twenty-five years there will be more Christians in Africa than in either Europe or North America. Christianity is also exploding in the heartlands of Hinduism, Buddhism, and Chinese religions. In these contexts the very word "Christian" carries strong connotations of Western culture or foreignness. For many, the words "Christian" and "church" call to mind Western imperialism or colonialism or worse. In short, the phrase "Christian church" can carry very negative cultural connotations, whereas the name "Christ" may not. This reality has caused many to rethink the very nature of the church as it has been known in the Christian West. This reexamination of ecclesiology is certainly a welcome and important development, since the doctrine has often become unnecessarily tethered to Western expressions of the church, which may not be appropriate for the growing church in the non-Western world. The focus of this article is on the emerging and growing phenomenon known as churchless Christianity, which is one response to the church as it has brought the Gospel to the non-Western world.

In his book *Churchless Christianity*, Herbert Hoefer has compiled data from people living in rural Tamil Nadu, India, and in its capital, urban Chennai (formerly Madras), who are devoted followers of Christ but who have not joined a visible Christian church and, indeed, remain within the Hindu community. Hoefer does not call them Christians but *Jesu bhakta*, that is, devotees of Jesus. This is no small movement. Hoefer's research suggests that there are more nonbaptized followers of Jesus in Chennai than there are formal, visible Christians in the traditional sense.[3] The Hindu *bhakti* movement allows Hindus to focus their worship on a particular god, so it is not scandalizing to the Hindu community for a Hindu to choose to worship Jesus, even exclusively Jesus. These *Jesu bhakta* follow an *ishta devata* (i.e., "chosen [*or* favorite] deity") theology and thereby maintain their cultural and social particularities as Hindus.[4] If asked, they identify themselves as Hindus, not as Christians, and many do not attend any church.[5] This unwillingness to identify with the church or with baptism is due, according to Hoefer, not to any shame about following Christ but to strong cultural associations surrounding the terms.

During a two-year period (2001–03), I surveyed the perceptions of Hindus in northern India regarding the church and Christianity.[6] I found that many Hindus do indeed have distorted and unfortunate associations with the notion of the church or organized Christianity. Hindus, for example, view Christians as disrespectful because they keep their shoes on during services of worship. They often look on Christians as culturally foreign because they sit on pews rather than on the floor, or use Western musical forms rather than *bhajans*, the indigenous forms of music in India. They simply do not understand why Christian women will no longer wear bangles or participate in popular cultural festivals. In short, even if Hindus are drawn to Christ, they may find membership in the church or the very word "Christian" repugnant. This negative association with the visible church raises the vital question, Can someone say yes to Jesus and no to the visible church?

Distorted associations with the terms "church" and "Christianity" are not limited to India, nor is the phenomenon of nonbaptized followers of Jesus who do not identify with the visible church. This pattern has also been observed throughout the Muslim world. Robby Butler tells the story of a Kuwaiti Muslim who was asked what he knew about Christians and Christianity. He replied that a Christian is someone who promotes immorality, pornography, and television programs like *Dallas* or *Sex in the City*. Butler goes on to comment that "for a Muslim to say that he has become a Christian is to communicate that he has launched into a secret life of immorality."[7] Within the Muslim community this embarrassing perception regarding words like "Christian," "church," and "Christianity" has also spawned churchless, but Christ-loving, movements. For example, Rafique Uddin and David Cashin have observed many Muslim followers of Jesus (Isa) who remain within the mosque, not uniting with a visible church.[8] *Mission Frontiers* highlighted a missionary couple, Alejandro and Bertha Ortiz, who have nurtured several of these "Jesus mosques" in Benin. They claim that another Muslim nation has over 100,000 Muslims who worship Jesus as Isa in Islamic mosques.[9]

This phenomenon raises some very important ecclesiological questions. For example, can a Hindu or a Muslim or a postmodern American disillusioned with the institutional church come to Jesus Christ, accept him as Lord and Savior, and *not* unite with the visible church?[10] Does someone have to use or accept the name "Christian" in order to belong to Christ? What is the meaning of baptism? Is it a public profession of one's *personal* faith in Christ, or does it also require incorporation into a *visible* community of believers? What is the relationship between ecclesiology and soteriology? Such questions cry out for further missiological reflection.

Historical Reference Points

It is essential that the whole discussion be explored with an appropriate historical perspective. We cannot properly evaluate the churchless Christianity movement without reference to several important milestones in the history of the church's understanding of ecclesiology. I do not question the *descriptive* truth of what Hoefer and others have documented. I am more interested, though, in whether the church has a *prescriptive* role in guiding and shaping this movement and in our response to it. To properly reflect on this history, we consider four historical reference points: the Nicene Creed, medieval Roman Catholic ecclesiology, the Reformation, and the creeds of later Protestantism.

Nicene Creed. One of the earliest ecclesiological statements embraced by the church is found in the Nicene Creed (A.D. 325): "I believe in one, holy, catholic, apostolic church." Two of these words are of particular significance to this discussion: "catholic" and "apostolic." Apostolicity may be in jeopardy if, for example, some churchless Christians continue to worship other gods besides Jesus or fail to embrace Trinitarianism.[11] Even if we suppose, however, that these churchless Christians are essentially orthodox in their doctrine, we still must ask about their recognition of the catholicity, or universality, of the church. Despite our many differences, catholicity reminds us that there is one Lord, one faith, and one baptism. Do nonbaptized followers of Jesus fully reflect the catholicity of the church? Are they an expression of the true mystery of catholicity, which defies all human organizational efforts, or do they represent a fracturing of the visible community of faith as it exists around the world, which, despite its many organizational and theological differences, nevertheless confesses Jesus as Lord in concert with other believers from around the world?

Medieval Roman Catholic ecclesiology. Popes in the Middle Ages—especially Innocent III at the Fourth Lateran Council in 1215 and Boniface VIII in 1302—identified salvation with being sacramentally connected to Christ through the church. This view traces back to the phrase *extra ecclesiam nulla salus* (outside the church there is no salvation), which Cyprian of Carthage (d. 258) coined in his *On the Unity of the Church* (251),[12] arguing that the doctrine was based on Jesus' words "Unless you eat the flesh of the Son of Man and drink his blood, you have no life in you" (John 6:53). The implication drawn was that not to receive the sacraments (baptism, absolution, the Eucharist, etc.) is to cut oneself off from Christ. The church is, to invoke a favorite patristic metaphor, like an ark. It is the vessel God has provided to save us from judgment. Those who enter into the ark are saved; those who do not, are lost.[13] From the traditional Catholic perspective, there is absolutely no room for an unbaptized follower of Christ who does not belong to Christ's holy church.[14]

The Reformation. The third ecclesiological reference point is the Reformation. One of the biggest theological challenges in the Reformation was to answer the objection that the movement seemed to be an assault on the catholicity of the church. As far back as Cyprian, the church fathers interpreted the church's unity as not merely mystical or invisible but episcopal. Cyprian gave us a second notable phrase: "He cannot have God for his father who has not the church for his mother."[15] The apostolic authority of the church was conveyed and continued through the episcopal laying on of hands from Peter to the present. The Reformation therefore represented a fracturing of the outward, visible unity of the Roman Catholic Church. It represented a challenge to the episcopal authority and thereby was viewed as schismatic and destructive of the Nicene marks of oneness, apostolicity, and catholicity.

Luther responded by rearticulating ecclesiology so that it was not tied to the structural and sacramental connection with a particular church organization; rather, it stressed the mystical communion of the saints that transcends all particular ecclesiastical organizations. The true church is apostolic, not because of an episcopal chain of the laying on of hands, but only when it teaches what the apostles taught. Protestant ecclesiology thus found its apostolic legitimacy through the doctrine of *sola Scriptura*. If the apostolic message is proclaimed, then the church is apostolic, and it shares in the mystical oneness and catholicity that are the marks of the true church. In his *On the Councils and the Churches*, Luther defines the true church as *sancta, catholica, Christiana*, that is, a Christian, holy people. Luther goes on to argue explicitly that when the Nicene Creed mentions "one holy, catholic, apostolic church," it refers to one holy, catholic, apostolic *people*.[16] The emphasis, he argued, has always been on the people of God, not the organizational structure to which they belonged. For Luther, the true, organic church has both a visible and an invisible nature. The visible church contains both unredeemed sinners and those who are saints by God's divine work. The invisible church, in contrast, consists of all true believers throughout time and space, the composition and number of which are known only to God.[17] Nevertheless, this Reformation articulation of a spiritual rather than episcopal basis for ecclesiology still finds its expression, however varied, in some visible expression of the church.

Later Protestant creedal formulation regarding the church. The fourth and final reference point emerges in the wake of the Reformation and is also pertinent to our evaluation of churchless Christianity. As the number of Reformation churches grew, a new crisis of ecclesiology developed because the initial protest from which we get our word "Protestant" did not fully anticipate the dizzying array of divisions, disputations, and controversies. Each new branch of Protestantism was forced to articulate its own understanding of the true marks of the church. The Augsburg Confession, for example, states that "the church is the assembly of saints in which the gospel is taught purely and the sacraments are administered rightly" (art. 7).[18] Similar words appear in the Thirty-nine Articles of the Church of England (art. 19).[19] The emerging Reformation churches tended to affirm the spiritual nature of the church, but they also set forth certain "marks" of the church, which could be embodied only in visible communities.

Conclusion. From a historical perspective, the existence of unbaptized believers in Christ who are not under the authority of the church is not accepted as normative ecclesiology. The traditional Catholic view that outside the church there is no salvation certainly would not accept the notion of followers of Jesus who are not in any sacramental relationship with the church. Similar statements could be found in the Eastern

Orthodox tradition.[20] The Reformation and the subsequent creedal formulations that speak to ecclesiology reveal that, despite a vigorous rethinking of the doctrine of the church, the Reformation churches could not possibly comprehend or accept a person untethered from the doctrine and discipline of the visible church. Indeed, virtually all Protestant churches have insisted on, as a minimum, the sacrament of baptism and the Lord's Supper as necessary signs of the visible church.[21] Most also insist on some organized authority of pastors, priests, bishops, or elders who preside over a defined, gathered community. Thus, if churchless Christianity is to be accepted, it clearly represents a departure from the historic doctrine of ecclesiology as espoused by Roman Catholic, Eastern Orthodox, and Protestant Christians.

Critique and Debate

Such a departure has been proposed by, among others, M. M. Thomas (1916–96), a well-known Indian theologian and ecumenical leader who for years was the director of the Christian Institute for the Study of Religion and Society, in Bangalore. The major critique of Thomas's ecclesiology was developed by Lesslie Newbigin (1909–98), British missionary to India, ecumenical leader, and bishop of the Church of South India. The result was a whole body of literature between these two men on the subject of ecclesiology, with many discussions on the nature of the church as a visible community. They each wrote dozens of books and articles.[22] The debate between Thomas and Newbigin on this issue remains the most sustained and theologically reflective discussion to date.

M. M. Thomas. In 1971 Thomas published a landmark book entitled *Salvation and Humanisation.* It is an examination of issues related to the theology of mission seen from within the particularities of the Indian context. Central to Thomas's vision is a radical rethinking of ecclesiology. Thomas is concerned with the implications of a church that becomes increasingly isolated from society. He therefore encourages the idea of a "Christ-centered secular fellowship outside the Church." He goes on to argue that a vigorous ecclesiology should embrace a view of the church that can "take form in all religious communities" because it "transcends all religious communities." Thomas would clearly embrace the notion of what Hoefer calls "churchless Christianity" but would rephrase it by saying that the church does not always exist as a defined, visible community but can be formed within other religious communities, such as

Hinduism and Islam. He states this point explicitly when he says that the church can "take form as a Christ-centered fellowship of faith and ethics in the Hindu religious community."[23] The fact that these followers of Jesus reject the sacrament of baptism is not, according to Thomas, because they do not wish to identify fully with Christ but because, in India, baptism has become "a sign not primarily of incorporation into Christ but of proselytism into a socio-political community involving rejection of their [own] socio-political-religious communities."[24] Since baptism as a "transfer of communal affiliation" is understood in India as an act of hostility toward one's own culture and social background, it makes a travesty of the true nature of baptism. Therefore, according to Thomas, at least in India we should not insist that the sacrament of baptism be considered a mark of the true church.

Thomas insists that there is a distinctive new humanity that belongs to Jesus Christ, but that this new humanity cannot be equated with the visible church. He says that "in spite of the famous slogan *extra ecclesiam nulla salus*," the new humanity of Christ does in fact exist outside the "empirical Church."[25] This is a new understanding of what might be called the invisible church. When Luther introduced the distinction of the invisible and visible church, it was for the purpose of acknowledging that there were unregenerate unbelievers who did not truly belong to Christ but who had become empirically united with the visible church on earth. Thomas is arguing the reverse situation. Namely, there are those who truly belong to Christ and thus are members of the invisible church in heaven but who have not united with any empirical, visible church on earth. Luther is concerned about unbelievers inside the visible church; Thomas is concerned with believers inside the visible community of Hinduism.

Lesslie Newbigin. In contrast, Lesslie Newbigin raises important questions about Thomas's ecclesiology. In *The Finality of Christ*, Newbigin insists that the church must involve a "visible community."[26] However, Newbigin wants to be clear that by "visible community" he is not merely embracing the notion that salvation in Christ is linked to mere "church extension" or the "aggrandizement of the community."[27] Instead, Newbigin argues that "a visible fellowship is central to God's plan of salvation in Christ; but God's plan of salvation is not limited to the visible fellowship." According to Newbigin, the proper balance is achieved when we realize that "true conversion involves *both* a new creation from above, which is not merely an act of extension of the existing community, and *also* a relationship with the existing community of believers." Thus, while acknowledging that salvation comes from God and is from above, central to God's plan of salvation is the uniting of his redeemed people to a visible community. So Newbigin directly responds to the churchless Christianity question when he says, quite bluntly: "Can a Hindu who has been born again in Christ by the work of the Holy Spirit be content to remain without any visible solidarity with his fellow-believers? The answer to that question is No. The New Testament knows nothing of a relationship with Christ which is purely mental and spiritual, unembodied in any of the structures of human relationship."[28]

Newbigin thus rejects what he regards as M. M. Thomas's overspiritualization of ecclesiology. For example, he asks, if someone belongs to a community sodality known as Hinduism, but at the same time confesses ultimate loyalty and allegiance to Jesus Christ, is it not naïve not to expect that there will be various points whereby commitment to Christ will "override his obligations as a Hindu, [and that] this allegiance must take visible—that is, social—forms?"[29] Furthermore, presumably "the acceptance of Jesus Christ as central and decisive creates *some* kind of solidarity among those who have this acceptance in common. If it did not do so, it would mean nothing. The question is, what is the nature of this solidarity? It has always been understood to include the practice of meeting together to celebrate with words, songs and formal actions the common faith in Jesus. . . . A man who is religiously, culturally and socially part of the Hindu community is a Hindu."[30]

The value of the Thomas-Newbigin debate lies both in the clarity with which each man states his views and in the depth of their theological reflection. Indeed, good biblical exegesis united with solid historical and theological reflection must be the ultimate arbiter of this debate.

Other voices. The most prominent contemporary missiologist to weigh in on this debate is Ralph Winter, the founder and director of the U.S. Center for World Mission, in Pasadena, California. Winter has made numerous statements in favor of the churchless Christianity movement. His comments suggest that, for him, churchless Christianity is not only missiologically sound but also strategically superior to traditional churches. Winter says, "Apparently, our real challenge is no longer to extend the boundaries of Christianity but to acknowledge that Biblical, Christian faith has already extensively flowed beyond Christianity as a cultural movement, just as it has historically flowed beyond Judaism and Roman Catholicism. Our task may well be to allow and encourage

Muslims and Hindus and Chinese to follow Christ without identifying themselves with a foreign religion. The Third Reformation is here!"[31] Winter's allusion to the Reformation is significant. If the first reformation was to move beyond the monocultural framework of Judaism and the second was to move beyond Roman Catholicism, this third reformation is churchless Christianity. Winter argues that we must now embrace the fact that the Gospel has already moved beyond explicitly identifiable Christian communities and can now exist, and even prosper, within the communities and structural framework of non-Christian religions.[32]

We thus have a body of evangelical scholars such as Ralph Winter, Herbert Hoefer, and H. L. Richard (author of *Following Jesus in the Hindu Context*[33]) who are increasingly siding with M. M. Thomas's new ecclesiology. It is therefore increasingly important for evangelical theologians to assess whether this new ecclesiology should be embraced by evangelical missiologists and by the missionary community as a whole, whether working among Muslims (Jesus Mosques), Hindus (Jesus Bhaktas) or postmodern Westerners (cyberchurch).

An Evangelical Missiologist's Response

I offer here an exploratory response to the issue of churchless Christianity. While generally supportive of many of the contributions and insights of these writers, I have some reservations about endorsing a churchless Christianity along the lines suggested by M. M. Thomas and H. L. Richard. To Richard's credit, he has called for a more vigorous debate on this issue.[34] To that end, I offer several points that I trust will promote a more sustained discussion of this issue.

Conversion, church, and community. First, to separate Christian conversion from visible Christian community is to separate two things that God has joined together. The word "church" (*ekklēsia*) in reference to the Christian community was inaugurated by Jesus Christ himself. To the charge that Jesus' use of the word "church" is only spiritual and not referring necessarily to a visible community, I reply that the very word *ekklēsia* means "public assembly." The choice of this word helped to launch the church as a visible, defined community into the world.

Notice, furthermore, that the defining confession of the Christian faith by Peter recorded in Matthew 16:16 is immediately linked to the necessity of community. Furthermore, this encounter took place in the pluralistic, multireligious context of Caesarea Philippi. After Peter's declaration, Jesus stated, "On this rock I will *build my church*" (Matt. 16:18).

Westernized Christianity versus churchless Christianity. Second, the discussion about churchless Christianity often creates the notion that the choice is between a Westernized Christianity and a churchless Christianity within some other religious community. In this scenario, it is easy to knock down the straw man of a Westernized Christianity. H. L. Richard correctly points out that the emerging Gentile Christianity found some within the Jerusalem church hostile to them, and yet God was clearly blessing the new movement. He is certainly correct in expressing his frustration about Christian communalism, legalistic sectarianism, separatist cultural attitudes, rigidity among Christian communities, and similar errors. However, that is like pointing out a thousand examples of bad and fragmented marriages as a reason to jettison the institution of marriage.

India has tens of thousands of churches all across the country whose members *do* sing Christian *bhajans* and not Westernized hymns, who *do* take their shoes off and sit on the floor rather than in pews, and who do not think twice about their women wearing bangles or participating in cultural festivals. But these are distinct, defined Christian communities that have existed for centuries in India.[35] The churchless Christians should, in my view, be baptized and then, as members of a global movement (even if they continue to reject Westernized forms of worship), find creative ways to express their catholicity with the global church.

Community and apostolicity. Third, the church is the divinely ordained institution that links believers to one another for correction, training in righteousness, and preserving the apostolic message. In a passage peculiar to Matthew's gospel, Jesus speaks about the role of the church in administering church discipline, which is the biblical basis for the wide acknowledgment of church discipline as a mark of the true church in the Protestant creedal tradition (Matt. 18:15–17). It is clear that the church exercises an important role in disciplining and defending the moral and doctrinal purity of the Christian community. Yet, how can church discipline be properly addressed in the context of churchless Christianity? What is the social context through which an Indian Christian who serves as an elder in a visible Christian community can confront or rebuke an erring *Jesu bhakta* woman who, for example, continues to go to Hindu temples to perform *puja* (worship) to Ganesh or Krishna alongside of her worship of Jesus Christ? This elder has no acknowledged authority over the life, faith, and practice of this *Jesu bhakta*, and as a man it would be almost impossible to find a culturally acceptable avenue through which he could meet with her and discuss her life and faith. Only the visible community provides the social structures that are essential to Christian discipleship in this context.

Ontic expansion of Christ. Finally, I am concerned that those of us in various visible communities around the world will not be able to properly benefit from the beauty of Christ that is uniquely manifested in the lives of these new believers. When the Gospel was first preached in the first century, it was confined to a single Jewish ethnic group. However, as the Gospel expanded and translated itself into Hellenistic culture and later into Chinese, Indian, African, Korean, and other cultures, we gained more insights into the beauty and reality of Jesus Christ. This phenomenon has been referred to as the ontic expansion of God in Jesus Christ. This reference is not to any ontological change in Jesus Christ. Nevertheless, our understanding and insight into the full nature of God in Jesus Christ is continually expanding as more and more people groups come to the feet of Jesus. This is the meaning behind the popular phrase "It takes a whole world to understand a whole Christ." We in the West have glaring blind spots that need to be illuminated by these *Jesu bhaktas* and followers of Isa within mosques. Perhaps our very understanding of the church does need to be broadened in certain areas. But practically speaking, none of this is possible if all believers in Jesus do not belong to some visible, defined community.

We worship a triune God who is, by nature, a relational God. He made his relational nature fully public in the incarnation of his Son, which is reflected in the life of the church, which in turn is called his body. Our very doctrine of Christ thus demands that all believers, in all times, in all parts of the globe must seek—whenever possible—to form themselves into visible communities of faith. The visible communities may have to meet in catacombs or suffer great persecution or undergo cultural misunderstanding, as did the primitive church, but the early church did not forsake the assembling of themselves together. They understood that biblical conversion, by definition, implies community.

Conclusion. There is no doubt that more creative thinking is needed if we are to effectively communicate the Christian Gospel into new global contexts. More vigorous discussion is needed on all of these issues. We also must not confuse the roles of description and prescription in responding to these developments. Finally, we must allow Scripture and history to guide and direct our thinking on this vital issue.

Notes

1. Philip Jenkins, *The Next Christendom: The Coming of Global Christianity* (New York: Oxford Univ. Press, 2002). See also Dana L. Robert, "Shifting Southward: Global Christianity Since 1945," *International Bulletin of Missionary Research* 24 (2000): 50–58.
2. Jenkins, *Next Christendom*, pp. 89, 90.
3. Herbert Hoefer, *Churchless Christianity*, new ed. (Pasadena, Calif.: William Carey Library, 2001; orig. pub., 1991), p. 96. Hoefer mentions 156,000 "nonbaptized believers in Christ" (30,000 high caste, i.e., Brahmin; 70,000 middle castes, i.e., Kshyatriya and Vaisya; and 56,000 scheduled castes, i.e., Sudra and Dalit); see appendixes 2–5, pp. 277–352.
4. The practice of *ishta devata* in Hinduism allows a person to worship a particular chosen deity without necessarily denying that other gods exist.
5. Some will occasionally make a pilgrimage to a large church, in the same way that Hindus make periodic pilgrimages to great temples in India.
6. This research has been published in English and in Hindi as *Your Questions—Our Answers* (Dehra Dun: Micropress, 2004), by Dharmanand Premraj (the author's pen name).
7. Robby Butler, "Unlocking Islam," *Mission Frontiers*, January–March 1991, p. 24. (*Mission Frontiers* is a publication of the U.S. Center for World Mission, Pasadena, Calif.)
8. Rafique Uddin, "Contextualized Worship and Witness," in *Muslims and Christians on the Emmaus Road*, ed. J. Dudley Woodberry (Monrovia, Calif.: MARC, 1989), pp. 267–72. On page 270 in particular Rafique Uddin summarizes his view when he states that the Muslim background believer in Christ should "stay within the frame of reference of Islamic worship, changing the inner values and meanings of the worship to fit his faith in Christ."
9. Erich Bridges, "Of 'Jesus Mosques' and Muslim Christians," *Mission Frontiers*, July–October 1997, p. 19. (*Mission Frontiers* reprinted this article from *The Commission* [August 1997], a publication of the International Mission Board of the Southern Baptist Convention.)
10. It should be noted that this issue is not limited to the non-Western World. For example, the Pew Internet and American Life Project (an initiative of the Pew Research Center) identified 28 million people in the U.S. alone who use the Internet for religious and spiritual information. Andrew Lord in "Virtual Communities and Mission" cites a Barna Research Group survey which suggests that "by 2010 we will probably have 10% to 20% of the population relying primarily or exclusively upon the internet for its religious

input" (*Evangelical Review of Theology* 26, no. 3 [2002]: 204). See also Michael L. Keene, "The Church on the Web," *Christian Century*, April 11–18, 1999, pp. 774–75.

11. Hoefer has surveyed the range of theological orthodoxy among certain clusters of churchless Christians. See his "Follow-up Reflections on 'Churchless Christianity,'" *Mission Frontiers*, March–April, 1999, pp. 36–41.

12. Cyprian of Carthage, *Epistle* 72.21. See also Cyprian, *Treatise* 1. See Alexander Roberts and James Donaldson, eds., *Ante-Nicene Fathers* (reprint, Peabody, Mass.: Hendrickson, 1999) (henceforth *Ante-Nicene Fathers*), 5:384, 421–29.

13. Cyprian, *Epistle* 74.15. See *Ante-Nicene Fathers*, 5:394. See also Jaroslav Pelikan, *The Emergence of the Catholic Tradition (100–600)* (Chicago: Univ. of Chicago Press, 1971), pp. 157, 158.

14. In the post–Vatican II era of Roman Catholicism, this teaching has been challenged, especially in the writings of Karl Rahner, who espoused implicit or "anonymous" Christianity, which is, quite clearly, untethered from either baptism or membership in any visible church. According to Vatican II, "Those who, through no fault of their own, do not know the Gospel of Christ or his Church, but who nevertheless seek God with a sincere heart, and, moved by grace, try in their actions to do his will as they know it through the dictates of their conscience—those too may achieve eternal salvation." See *Lumen gentium*, Dogmatic Constitution on the Church, sec. 16.

15. The Treatises of Cyprian, *The Unity of the Catholic Church* 6. See *Ante-Nicene Fathers*, 5:423.

16. *Works of Martin Luther*, 5:264–66, as quoted in Hugh T. Kerr, ed., *A Compend of Luther's Theology* (Philadelphia: Westminster Press, 1966), pp. 124, 125.

17. Luther's concept of the invisible church was widely accepted in Protestant ecclesiology, as is reflected in a wide range of confessional documents. See, for example, the First Scottish Confession (1560), Westminster Confession (1647), Savoy Declaration (1658), and Philadelphia Baptist Confession (1688). These confessions can be found in Philip Schaff, ed., *The Creeds of Christendom*, 3 vols. (Grand Rapids: Baker, 1983).

18. *The Book of Concord: The Confessions of the Evangelical Lutheran Church*, ed. Robert Kolb and Timothy J. Wengert (Minneapolis: Fortress Press, 2000), p. 43.

19. Philip Schaff, ed., *The Creeds of Christendom*, vol. 3 (Grand Rapids: Baker, 1983), p. 499.

20. See Dumitru Staniloae, *Theology and the Church* (Crestwood, N.Y.: St. Vladimir's Seminary Press, 1980).

21. Even the twelfth-century Waldenses, who were one of the earliest groups to rebel against papal authority, affirmed the essential nature of the sacraments. See Confession of the Waldenses (1655), art. 28, as quoted in Schaff, *Creeds of Christendom*, p. 765.

22. A bibliography of the key documents related to this debate between Newbigin and Thomas appears in George R. Hunsberger, "Conversion

and Community: Revisiting the Lesslie Newbigin–M. M. Thomas Debate,"
International Bulletin of Missionary Research 22 (1998): 112–17.

23. M. M. Thomas, *Salvation and Humanisation* (Madras: CLS, 1971), pp. 13, 38,
40. Thomas cites Keshub Chunder Sen as one who modeled this possibility
through his Church of the New Dispensation.

24. M. M. Thomas, "Baptism, the Church, and Koinonia," *Religion and Society*
19, no. 1 (1972): 73.

25. Ibid., p. 71.

26. Lesslie Newbigin, *The Finality of Christ* (London: SCM Press, 1969), p. 96.

27. Hunsberger, "Conversion and Community," p. 112.

28. Newbigin, *The Finality of Christ*, pp. 97, 107, 106 (emphasis in original).

29. Hunsberger, "Conversion and Community," p. 115, quoting Newbigin.

30. Lesslie Newbigin, "Baptism, the Church, and Koinonia," *Religion and Society*
19, no. 1 (1972): 78.

31. Ralph Winter, "Eleven Frontiers of Perspective," *International Journal of
Frontier Missions* 20, no. 4 (2003): 136.

32. Winter's imprecise language may incorrectly lead the reader to assume
that he is merely stating that Christian growth cannot be identified with
organizational aggrandizement or that we should avoid introducing new
Hindu background believers to a "foreign religion." The context of his
reflections make it clear, however, that he is enthusiastic about "churchless
Christianity," as described by Thomas and Hoefer.

33. H. L. Richard, *Following Jesus in the Hindu Context: The Life and Legacy of
N. V. Tilak* (Pasadena, Calif.: William Carey Library, 1999).

34. Richard states, "In the eight years since the publication of *Churchless
Christianity* little notice seems to have been taken, debate has not been
stirred and, most tragically, ministry strategies that affirm and empower the
NBBC [non-baptized believers in Christ] have not yet been born. Yet this is
a book that demands debate and response. But where and by whom might
this begin?" See H. L. Richard, "Christ-Followers in India Flourishing—but
Outside the Church," *Mission Frontiers*, January 2000 (special Hindu ed.),
p. 19.

35. Robert de Nobili, for example, a Jesuit missionary in India, propagated
Christianity within the very strict boundaries of Brahminic social customs
in the early seventeenth century.

8

Mission and Proselytism:
A Middle East Perspective

David A. Kerr

The approximately 10–12 million Christians of West Asia / North Africa (i.e., of the so-called Middle East) represent a kaleidoscope of Christian churches and cultural traditions.[1] The great majority are Orthodox members of the Oriental and Eastern Orthodox churches, which account for more than 75 percent of the total Christian population of the region. Catholic churches of both Eastern and Western (Latin) rites account for about another 20 percent. The evangelical or Protestant churches form a minority of between 3 and 4 percent.[2] These figures, based on David Barrett's calculations, relate to the churches that are today members of the Middle East Council of Churches (MECC), probably the world's most inclusive regional ecumenical council. Successor to the predominantly Protestant Near East Council of Churches, it embraces four families of churches (Oriental Orthodox, Eastern Orthodox, Catholic, and Protestant), with the Assyrian Church of the East (so-called Nestorian) possibly joining in the future as a fifth family.[3]

This ecumenical achievement is a positive sign of reconciliation between the indigenous churches, which for centuries have lived in disunity and mutual mistrust. It expresses their growing willingness to resolve historical problems of division by a concerted witness to the Gospel's power of renewal and reconciliation in a politically torn region.

Among the ecclesial issues on the MECC agenda is the problem of proselytism. This was the subject of a special report, "Proselytism, Sects, and Pastoral Challenges: A Study Document," which the Commission on Faith and Unity prepared for the MECC's Fifth General Assembly in 1989.[4] As the most ecumenical document on the issue in the West Asian / North African perspective, it provides an appropriate starting point for this essay.

Proselytism: The MECC Definition

The MECC study document defines proselytism as "a practice that involves attempts aimed at attracting Christians from a particular Church or religious group, leading to their alienation from their Church of origin." It is treated as an issue of ecumenical malpractice that contravenes biblical understandings of how God relates to humankind, how Christians relate to one another, and respect for the human right to be free from coercion in religious matters. The problem is analyzed as having psychological roots in "individual and group egoism," political manifestations in "feelings of cultural, political and economic superiority," and institutional dimensions in "an overtrust in one's present methods and programmes." It is perpetuated by ignorance of Christian traditions other than those of one's own cultural or political background, and it may include the willful "dissimulation of the truth about them." Proselytism is therefore seen as the opposite of authentic evangelism, which emphasizes "confidence in God and His economy" as the basis of mission.[5]

The MECC document addresses two dimensions of the issue. In historical terms it is related to the "western missionary strategy" of the medieval Catholic missions and their Protestant successors.[6] The contemporary dimension is identified mainly with "sects"—by which the MECC means millenarian or messianic groups, independent "neo-missionary" groups of fundamentalist persuasions, groups that represent syncretistic forms of religious universalism, charismatic renewal movements within established churches, and new religious movements that claim to draw upon Asian forms of religious spirituality.[7] While proselytism in West Asia / North Africa occurs unconsciously as well as consciously, its underlying presupposition is that a missionary "vacuum" exists throughout the region, where indigenous churches are considered to be lacking missionary motivation and resources.[8]

With this understanding of proselytism, the present essay will examine manifestations of the problem in the complex history of the Eastern churches' experience of the Western church and its missions. It will then review contemporary initiatives in intra-Christian dialogue, one of the benefits of which has been the emergence of a clearer understanding of how the Orthodox churches understand Christian witness. Attention will be given to the MECC's suggested remedies, and in conclusion we shall examine some of the contextual issues that shape the identity of Eastern churches.

Historical Dimensions

Eastern patriarchates. For the indigenous West Asian / North African Christian communities, it is a matter of historic pride and contemporary self-understanding that Christianity has been continuously present throughout the region since apostolic times. The cities of Jerusalem, Antioch, Alexandria, and Etchmiadzin are quite as important for Christians as are Mecca, Medina, and Jerusalem for Muslims, and Jerusalem for Jews. They are the places where the apostles proclaimed the Gospel and founded the first churches that carried forward the Christian mission.

In ecclesiastical language, they constitute the "patriarchates" of the East. They have always seen themselves as existing in an equal apostolic relationship with the Western patriarchates of Rome and Constantinople. From the fourth century, Rome was accorded a spiritual primacy as *primus inter pares*, though without the universal authority that Catholics later invested in the papacy. Constantinople (originally known by its Greek pre-Christian name of Byzantium) held political primacy within the Byzantine Empire, to which most of the Eastern churches belonged. But in ecclesial terms the Easterners have always insisted on the coequal autonomy of each patriarchate as the institutional reality of the biblical conception of the universal church; as the human body is made up of many members, so the apostolic churches are the members of the body of Christ.

The patriarchates have always been the centers of Eastern Christian liturgy, theology, witness, and church administration, expressed in their ancient ethnic languages (Syriac and Aramaic in Antioch and Jerusalem; Coptic in Alexandria). This continued to be true long after the seventh century, when the rise of Islam, its military conquests, and the extension of its political power under the Islamic caliphate reduced the Eastern patriarchates socially to the role of Christian minorities in increasingly Muslim societies.

To the northeastern frontier of the Byzantine Empire lay the kingdom of Armenia. Here the church traces its foundation to the apostles Thaddeus and Bartholemew. The Armenian monarchy recognized Christianity as the national religion from the beginning of the fourth century, even before the conversion of the Byzantine emperor Constantine.[9] Armenian Christians have ever since looked to Etchmiadzin as the seat of what they call their "catholicosate," which, in terms of Armenian canon law, has higher authority than a patriarchate.[10]

Despite the diversity of cultural, linguistic, and social characteristics that they represented, the five patriarchates and the Armenian catholicosate preserved the common faith of the Nicene Creed (325) until the early fifth century. This is remembered as the period of "the undivided church." Over the following centuries this ecumenical fellowship proved vulnerable to centrifugal forces. The ecumenical Council of Ephesus (431) excommunicated the Eastern members of the patriarchate of Antioch. To escape the persecution of those whom the Byzantine rulers declared heretics, these Assyrian Christians took refuge in Persia.[11] Twenty years later the Council of Chalcedon (451) witnessed doctrinal cleavage between the Copts (Egyptians) of Alexandria, the remaining Syrians of Antioch, and the Armenians of Etchmiadzin on the one hand, and the churches of Constantinople and Rome on the other.[12]

Oriental Orthodox. Since Chalcedon, the Copts, Syrians, and Armenians, together with the church of Kerala (India) and the church of Ethiopia, have formed the family of Oriental Orthodox churches. They are "autocephalous," or self-governing, but united in creed and liturgy. Each is inseparably identified with the people and culture in which it exists and in this sense can be described sociologically as ethnic churches. Contextually, this characteristic has been a source of strength throughout their histories and helps explain their remarkable tenacity to the Christian faith, despite their being under Islamic rule. Their numerical decline through the medieval centuries did not diminish the quality of their spiritual life, which is evident in a wealth of theological writing and liturgical expression.[13] Today they continue to account for the majority of West Asian and North African Christians.

Eastern Orthodox. After the Chalcedonian separation, smaller communities of Christians in Antioch and Alexandria remained in communion with Constantinople and technically with Rome. Often referred to as Melkites (from Arabic *malik*, meaning "king," in reference to the Byzantine emperor), their orthodoxy is of the Chalcedonian kind. In MECC ecumenical parlance they constitute the Eastern Orthodox family. Historically their presence has been strongest in the cosmopolitan coastal regions of West Asia and North Africa. Though historical links with the Greek church continue, especially in the patriarchate of Jerusalem, the Eastern Orthodox patriarchate of Antioch identifies itself as the church of the Arabs.[14] It has contributed in diverse ways to the development in the nineteenth and twentieth centuries of Arab nationalism and is committed to social coexistence with Islam. Relations between the Eastern and Oriental Orthodox, though strained in the past, have grown more intimate through a series of pan-Orthodox conferences that began in Addis Ababa in 1965.

Eastern Catholics. This historical survey has so far exposed factors that resulted in the disunity of the Eastern churches. The refusal of one church to recognize the ecclesial validity of another is the soil in which proselytism is seeded. It was with the extension of Western Catholicism into West Asia, in consequence of Rome's denial of the ecclesial integrity of the Eastern patriarchates under what it deemed as their heretical doctrines, that the growth of proselytism began.

To avoid generalization, it is important to emphasize at the outset of this discussion that the oldest and largest indigenous community of West Asian Catholics is the Maronites. Exactly as we have seen to be the case with the Oriental and Eastern Orthodox sense of ethnic identity, the Maronites have strong ethnic ties to Lebanon, where land and faith have combined in the Maronite sense of being a national church. Their union with Rome was gradually consolidated from the era of the Latin Crusades (between the eleventh and thirteenth centuries), and though their ecclesiastical customs were subject to extensive Latinization, they never lost their original Syriac identity, which today they often proudly reaffirm.

In contrast to the Maronites, who claim to have been Catholic from their origins between the fifth and seventh centuries, other Catholic communities have sprung up as the result of the later missionary activity of the Western Catholic church. Following the mutual anathemas exchanged between Rome and Constantinople in 1054 and the subsequent failure of the Council of Ferrara-Florence (1437–39) to heal the rift between Latin Catholicism and Eastern Orthodoxy, the Catholic Church developed a strategy for reunion with the East by the conversion of the Oriental and Eastern Orthodox churches to Catholicism. Western Catholic missions, initially led by the Franciscans and later by the Jesuits, exerted a powerful Latinizing influence upon the Maronites and won converts from the other churches. Thus, corresponding to each Oriental and Eastern Orthodox church, a Catholic equivalent arose: Chaldean (Assyrian) Catholic (1553), Syrian Catholic (1663), Melkite (Greek) Catholic (1724), Armenian Catholic (1742), and Coptic Catholic (1895). By recognizing these convert churches as the canonical heirs of the ancient Eastern patriarchates, Rome claimed to be reuniting the church.[15] Together with the Latin Catholic Patriarchate of Jerusalem,[16] these Catholic patriarchates are defined by the Second Vatican Council as part of "the divinely revealed and undivided heritage of the universal Church."[17]

The Vatican designates these churches as Eastern-rite Catholics, in distinction from the Roman (or Latin) Catholic rite of the West. This label emphasizes the Catholic view that they enrich the universal Catholic Church by preserving distinctive elements of their original canonical traditions. Their alternative designation as "Uniate" churches (i.e., united with Rome), while having long historical currency, emphasizes rather the fact of their conversion, which incurs the Eastern and Oriental Orthodox charge of proselytism. The very existence of these churches is therefore problematic; what the Catholics have regarded as a symbol of reunion, the Orthodox have treated as "a major obstacle to the progress of the dialogue" with the Catholic Church.[18] The fact that significant progress has recently been made in this dialogue is an ecumenical achievement to which we shall return later in this article.

Evangelical churches. In the nineteenth century, Eastern churches, led by the Maronites, joined cause in laying the charge of proselytism this time against the evangelical missions that had arrived in West Asia. In 1823 the first missionaries of the American Board of Commissioners for Foreign Mission (ABCFM) began evangelistic work in Beirut and Mount Lebanon. The Maronite patriarch greeted them with an encyclical that condemned their version of the Bible and forbade Maronites to associate with the English *bibliyyun* ("biblicists"). In May of that year, Pope Leo XII backed the patriarch by issuing a further condemnation of "a certain Bible society" which had printed and distributed a corrupt version of the Scriptures.[19]

The aim of the missionaries was the revival of "nominal Christians," who, by becoming "Christian in heart," were expected to advance the evangelization of Muslims and Jews. The initial ABCFM policy was stated by Rufus Anderson as follows: "not to subvert them [the indigenous churches]; not to pull them down and build anew. It is to reform them; to revive among them . . . the knowledge and spirit of the Gospel. . . . It is not part of our object to introduce Congregationalism or Presbyterianism among them. . . . We are content that their present ecclesiastical organization should remain, provided the knowledge and spirit of the Gospel can be revived under it."[20]

This statement did not prevent the emergence of separate evangelical churches. Some of the missionaries found it impossible to credit the indigenous churches with any spiritual vitality.[21] Orthodox and Catholic Christians who associated with the evangelical missionaries were ostracized by their church hierarchies, the case of the Maronite As'ad Shidyaq becoming the cause célèbre when he was imprisoned by the Maronite patriarch and died in jail (ca. 1823).[22] When in 1826 two Armenians, Gregory Wortabet and Dionysius Carabet, asked to be received into an evangelical fellowship, the missionaries decided to form themselves into a church.

The first evangelical church was established in Beirut. "Being desirous of enjoying Christian ordinances," its founding members determined (in the words of their charter) "to adopt with some variations, the Articles of Faith and the Form of Covenant, used by the First Church in Hartford in Connecticut, U.S.A., to be publicly read on the admission of members."[23] Increase in the number of converts during the mid-nineteenth century and the need for an appropriate form of institutional organization within the Ottoman millet system of religious communities encouraged the missionaries to develop a fourfold policy: the conversion of indigenous "nominal" Christians, the organization of convert evangelical churches, the training of an indigenous ministry, and the publication of Christian literature.[24] Anderson acquiesced in the missionaries' practice as a result of his 1844 visit through the region, and his original policy of nonproselytism evolved to "the restoration of pre-Constantinian and primitive (Pauline) Christianity . . . [by] the formation not only of exemplary individuals in their [i.e., the Eastern churches'] midst but of exemplary communities as well."[25] But he recognized the consequence of this policy change when he later wrote: "This admission of converts into a church, without regard to their previous ecclesiastical relation, was a practical ignoring of the old church organizations in that region. It was so understood, and the spirit of opposition and persecution was roused to the utmost."[26]

The ABCFM policy in this regard is but a concise example of the practice of the nineteenth-century Anglican, Lutheran, and Reformed missions in Turkey, Palestine, and Egypt. An Anglican bishopric was established in Jerusalem in 1841 largely through the efforts of Britain's Church Missionary Society. German missionaries created the Evangelical Lutheran Church of Jordan around 1860. In addition to the work of the ABCFM in Lebanon, which gave rise to the present National Evangelical Synod of Syria and Lebanon, its activity in Turkey spawned an Armenian evangelical congregation in 1846, which has grown to become the Union of the Armenian Evangelical Churches in the Near East. American Presbyterians in Cairo founded the Coptic Evangelical Church in 1853, which is today the largest and most influential Protestant denomination in the region.[27]

In his discussion of the evangelical churches of West Asia, Norman Horner notes that "the vast majority of their membership came originally from Orthodox and Eastern-rite Catholic churches. This has left a residue of mutual suspicion and ill will that can be overcome only by more creative ecumenical relationships than yet exist, especially between Protestant and Orthodox churches."[28]

Intra-Christian Dialogue

Our overview of centuries of church history in the West Asian / North African region will have served its purpose if it illustrates the ubiquity of intra-Christian proselytism as an issue with which the contemporary churches must deal. It sets discomforting questions against the cherished Western maxim that the modern ecumenical movement evolved from the history of missions. The Western trajectory of mission has been experienced as profoundly anti-ecumenical by the Eastern churches, compounding the disunity that already existed and arguably weakening the situation of Christian minorities within Muslim societies.

Against this background the ecumenical achievements of the MECC are the more remarkable. Mutual recognition among the different member families of churches has offset the absolutist demands that continue to be heard in other regions affected by similar historical problems (e.g., the demand by some Orthodox that Uniatism be abolished by the absorption of the Uniates into the Latin rite of Roman Catholicism).[29]

The process of healing these historical wounds can be illustrated by two significant examples, both of which have had a positive impact on the life of the MECC, though the initiatives originated elsewhere. The first involves the Catholic and Eastern Orthodox churches, which, since 1990, have been trying to resolve the issue of the Eastern-rite Catholic (Uniate) churches. Their joint "Statement on the Subject of Uniatism," published as the Freising Declaration of 1990, became the basis of a continuing dialogue in which it has been agreed that while the Eastern-rite Catholic churches have come into existence as part of the historic search for unity, Uniatism no longer provides a model or method for Catholic-Orthodox rapprochement. In the contemporary, ecumenical understanding of the church as a communion of those who receive the "gifts and graces" of the Holy Spirit,[30] neither Catholics nor Orthodox claim exclusive possession of the Holy Spirit's authenticating marks. They embrace one another as pilgrims in a Spirit-guided journey toward perfect communion. In this pilgrimage the Eastern-rite Catholics/Uniates serve not as intermediaries between sister churches but as fellow pilgrims who seek to make their own specific contribution to the growth of Christian koinonia.[31] Although a certain ambiguity remains about the specific ecumenical role of the Eastern-rite Catholics, agreement that Uniatism is no longer a model for ecclesial reunion represents a significant defusing of tensions created by proselytism.

A second example of intra-Christian dialogue is the growth since the late 1980s of bilateral conversations between Western evangelical missions and the indigenous churches of West Asia / North Africa. An annual conference of Evangelicals for Middle East Understanding (EMEU), founded in 1987, provides a framework for dialogue between indigenous Christians and Western evangelicals who are exploring cooperative rather than competitive understandings of mission. Speaking to evangelicals, EMEU director Donald Wagner calls for "a new day for mission . . . [in which] we must strive to become authentic partners with the churches of the Middle East. We will discover that God is already at work in Jerusalem, the West Bank, Beirut, Cairo, Baghdad, and throughout this region. We will not only learn from our sisters and brothers in the faith in these lands, but will find the true meaning of being the church in new ways that will honor the Lord and the gospel he gave us."[32]

An example of this sort of dialogue has been published in *Turning Over a New Leaf: Protestant Missions and the Orthodox Churches of the Middle East*. This book introduces Western evangelicals to the life of the indigenous churches of West Asia in a concise, informed, and sensitive manner that seeks to replace negative stereotypes by "a kinder, gentler understanding."[33] It explores aspects of Orthodox theology that evangelicals find difficult (e.g., works/faith relationship, the Eucharist, Mariology, the communion of saints, and apostolic succession) and develops a frank discussion of differences between their respective understandings of salvation and spiritual renewal. It is especially helpful in showing how Orthodox spiritual renewal draws inspiration from the Orthodox liturgy of worship.

These examples show evidence of a process of reconciliation at least between churches (Catholic-Orthodox) and mission groups

(Western evangelicals) whose understanding of mission centers upon the church and the local Christian community. It must be admitted, however, that these positive developments have little impact on those groups that, as noted above, the MECC terms "sects." From the EMEU perspective, Donald Wagner has expressed concern about what he sees as "the western orientation and cultural insensitivity" of the evangelical AD 2000 movement. He also subjects the theology and policies of the International Christian Embassy Jerusalem to critical scrutiny, concluding that it "allows the gospel and lordship of Jesus Christ to become subservient to the modem political ideology of Zionism . . . reducing the Christian church to a mere 'parenthesis' and rejecting the local Christian community."[34]

Orthodox Understandings of Mission

Perhaps the most sensitive issue for continuing dialogue between Western and Eastern churches is the nature of mission itself. On grounds that the ethnic identity of Eastern churches is assumed to deprive them of a real sense of mission, evangelicals sometimes continue the nineteenth-century practice of justifying a proselytizing evangelism of Eastern Christians so that they might become effective channels of indigenous evangelism. Orthodox response to being treated as *terra missionis* often caricatures Western missions as a continuation of the medieval crusades and has resulted in denunciation of the word "mission." With its Latin connotations of "sending forth," they associate mission negatively with their historic experience of the imperial ambitions of the Holy Roman Empire and its successor European states.

Orthodox churches generally prefer the Greek term *martyria* (witness). The following paragraphs attempt to summarize the content that modern Orthodox have given this term in their recent missiological writings and consultations.

Witness as liturgy. The heart of the Orthodox understanding of witness is the liturgy. "The Liturgy," writes Metropolitan Anastasios of Albania (formerly professor at the University of Athens), "is a continuous transformation of life according to the prototype Jesus Christ, through the power of the Spirit. If it is true that in the Liturgy we not only hear a message but we participate in the great event of liberation from sin and of *koinonia* (communion) with Christ through the real presence of the Holy Spirit, then this event of our personal incorporation into the Body of Christ, this transfiguration of our little being into a member of

Christ, must be evident and be proclaimed in actual life. The Liturgy has to be continued in personal, everyday situations. . . . Without this continuation the Liturgy remains incomplete."[35]

Liturgy after the Liturgy. The idea of continuity between the liturgy and witness in life is expressed in the phrase "liturgy after the Liturgy." Ion Bria, the Romanian Orthodox theologian who served as Orthodox adviser in the World Council of Churches' Commission on World Mission and Evangelism, explains it thus: "The mission of the Church rests upon the radiating and transforming power of the Liturgy. It is the stimulus in sending out the people of God to the world to confess the Gospel and to be involved in man's liberation."[36]

Liturgy as witness/mission means the church being in the midst of the human community it serves in order to transform it into the Christlike image and likeness of God (*theosis*). This necessitates the radical conversion of societies and individuals whose lives are characterized by sin, separation from God, and submission to the evils of idolatry (social and political as much as religious). Accordingly, a group of Orthodox theologians who met in Bucharest in 1974 to discuss the topic "Confessing Christ Today" analyzed witness under its "vertical" (divine-human) and "horizontal" (social-individual) dimensions. They emphasized that "the first method of evangelistic witness is the sharing of love by those who have acknowledged the love of God for them." They argued that this primary expression of witness, this self-giving quality of Christian lives that invite emulation, is a more effective way of transforming human communities than "the bold announcement of Christ as Saviour to a world which has already heard the words and still remains unresponsive."[37]

The context of witness. The ethnic and national identity of Orthodox churches means that the primary context of their witness is their own people and nations. For much of the twentieth century, Orthodox churches living under the restrictions of Communist regimes had no opportunity to witness beyond their own societies. But contemporary Orthodox theologians insist that their understanding of witness is not contingent on a particular sociopolitical circumstance. It flows from the Orthodox ecclesiology, which identifies the church with the people (*laos*) as "the people's church."[38] This understanding gives missiological priority to the indigenization of faith in a particular culture so that the latter is transformed by gospel values. The Orthodox consultation "Confessing Christ Today" identified four dimensions of such indigenous evangelization: (1) the evangelization of those who are Christian in name but ignore their baptism either deliberately or through indifference; (2) the penetration of superficially Christian cultures with the transforming power of the Holy Spirit reaching into "every nook and cranny" of national life; (3) the evangelization of "the structures of this world," especially in the social, economic, and political spheres, where the church should give voice to the poor and oppressed; and (4) the evangelization of secularized men and women for whom transcendence, forgiveness, and the sacramental have no meaning.[39]

Evangelism. The notion of the people's church must at the same time be understood within the historic order of the ministries within the Orthodox Church. The primary evangelists are the bishops, their presbyters and deacons, and the monastic orders. The monastic community has the specific evangelistic role of living as "a sign, a paradigm, an anticipation and foretaste of the Kingdom," sanctifying time and seeking the renewal of the inner life through unceasing prayer.[40] Modern Orthodoxy is rediscovering the power of the laity, especially through the development of various Orthodox youth movements. Given the persecution that many Orthodox churches have experienced from hostile political authorities, it is important to recognize the evangelistic value of the faithful who suddenly find themselves called to physical martyrdom. Evangelism, therefore, while the calling of the whole church, is effectively exercised by particular representatives who witness "from within the faith and truth of the body of the Church."[41]

Cross-cultural witness. The Orthodox churches' firm emphasis on culturally indigenized witness may seem to beg the question, often asked by Western missionaries, of the place of cross-cultural witnessing in Orthodox priorities. However, Orthodox history proudly records the evangelization of the Slavs by the ninth-century Greek brothers Saints Cyril and Methodius. This century has seen innovative forms of intra-Orthodox missionary cooperation in Africa, Alaska, and the Far East, regions of what is sometimes called the Orthodox diaspora. Cross-cultural evangelism has not figured significantly in the witness of Orthodox churches living under restrictive political (e.g., the former Soviet Union and Eastern Europe) or socioreligious (e.g., Islam) conditions, which we have already acknowledged. Recent political change in Russia and Eastern Europe opens new opportunities, though the recurrence in Eastern Europe of previously suppressed animosities between Eastern-rite Catholics and Orthodox, on the one hand, and evangelicals and Orthodox, on the other, has revived Orthodox suspicions of mission as involving one church transgressing the ethnic context of another. Where cross-cultural evangelization is possible, Orthodox agree that its subjects must be non-Christians, not Christians from other Orthodox, Catholic, or evangelical churches.[42]

Christian witness within Islam. Since the seventh century, Islam has provided the social, cultural, and political framework of Orthodox presence in West Asia and North Africa. It exceeds the scope of this article to review this long history of Orthodox-Muslim relations.[43] The contribution of Father Joseph el-Zahlaoui, an Antiochian Orthodox living in Lebanon, to the compendium *Your Will Be Done: Orthodoxy in Mission* offers a good example of a contemporary Orthodox whose concern is with witness in the context of Islam.[44]

Rejecting the view that the Orthodox communities have been introverted by the social experience of Islam, el-Zahlaoui reminds us of important ways in which Orthodox Christians have contributed to the cultural, ideological, and scientific renaissance of Arab societies in different periods of their history. His general point is that "Christianity became an essential spiritual force in the cultural, social and political life of Arab Muslims."

The contemporary resurgence of conservative religious trends throughout the region confronts all minorities with difficult problems. Many Christians feel threatened, even to the point of fearing for their survival. As in previous times of crisis, many Christians opt to emigrate out of the region, usually to the West, with the result that the remaining Christian presence is seriously weakened. Hard as this situation makes it for many Christians to give confident witness, el-Zahlaoui insists on the responsibility of the church to relate the Gospel to this crisis. "The witness of the Gospel challenges us to transform the prevailing destructive suspicion between the minorities and majorities into constructive confidence."

In practical terms, this means that the church must identify with the cause of all victims of injustice in "a fidelity to Christ who calls us to assume on behalf of everybody all true human solidarity." In the Lebanese context el-Zahlaoui emphasizes the church's medicosocial and educational services, through which it witnesses the presence of God within human suffering and manifests the reconciliatory power of the Incarnation.[45]

The most serious impediment to effective Christian witness is the disunity of Christian churches. "Where the Church should be a manifestation of God's love to all human beings and a united community in God's peace, it often appears as a gathering of sects, mutually exclusive of one another." Such disunity invites the criticism of Muslims whose scripture, the Qur'an, argues that disunity is a sign of God's punishment upon Christians who have neglected their divine covenant (5:15).[46] The challenge of Christian witness within Muslim societies, el-Zahlaoui concludes, demands concerted "spiritual and theological reflection on the meaning of our faith and of our beliefs in the Islamic context in which we live."[47]

A Pastoral Approach to Issues of Proselytism

The MECC document with which this essay began calls for "a pastoral agreement" among churches for the resolution of historical and contemporary problems of proselytism.[48] The key to this approach is "a dialogue of love"[49] in which Christians of different traditions learn to listen to one another in their search for mutual correction and enrichment. The examples we have given point to the growth of such dialogue between churches and with missionary agencies that operate with an ecclesial commitment, however varied this may be. The MECC study document lists several issues that call for discussion under the category of "unconscious" proselytism, such as religious freedom and the freedom of conscience, the issue of "returning to the mother church," mixed marriages and religious education, and the evangelization of nominal Christians.

Is dialogue possible with what the MECC terms "sects," for which, in its judgment, "proselytism is a constitutive element of their identity"? If the MECC has less confidence in dialogue in this respect, there being "not enough basis for a constructive dialogue," it nevertheless recommends "a pastoral strategy" that specifically rejects the option of trying to suppress the freedom of sects to operate. No haven is offered to the argument that civil law should be invoked against the sects. On the contrary, the study document insists that the freedom of the sects to operate must be upheld, as also the fight of the individual to choose his or her religious affiliation.[50]

A pastoral approach to the sects should include challenge in two senses of the word: challenge *to* the sects by monitoring their activities and raising "awareness of the religious and human threats of this phenomenon"; and the challenge *of* the sects, in that the churches should be energized for renewal, expressed in "a more efficient pastoral work that 'recaptures what has been lost' and immunizes [the] faithful against the temptations of 'religious consumerism.'" Without elaborating further, the document emphasizes the need for continuing renewal of religious education, ministerial formation, pastoral care, and "the balance between participation and the need for leadership" (which this author reads as meaning the new relationship between clergy and laity).

Issues for Intra-Christian Dialogue

The MECC's call for dialogue between Eastern and Western churches implicitly requires us to consider the sociopolitical context in which proselytism continues to evoke contentious argument. At least three dimensions of Christian identity need to be kept in mind.

Christian religious identity in West Asia / North Africa. The Lebanese theologian George Sabra reminds us that religion continues to function as a primary factor of social identity throughout the West Asian / North African region. He draws a helpful distinction between the "denominational" (or sociological) identity of a Christian community and the "ecclesial" (or faith) commitment of its members. These two dimensions may be continuous with each other. But modern forces of secularization have tended to erode the ecclesial vitality of many Christians who nonetheless continue to be socially defined by their denomination. In this context, Sabra argues, the purpose of evangelization is to enhance the ecclesial identity of individuals and communities. He then poses the question, If the faith renewal of an individual or group leads to a change of ecclesial affiliation, is this evangelization or proselytism?[51]

Two variables tend to influence the way this question is answered. Where continuity between church and ethnicity is strong (e.g., in the Oriental Orthodox churches and the Maronite church), change of ecclesial affiliation from the mother church is unconscionable and treated as a betrayal of community. In cases where ecclesiology has reduced or eliminated the sense of ethnicity (e.g., in Protestant churches), the quality of personal faith commitment/salvation is the primary value of evangelism.

Here the second variable becomes evident. Where faith is understood in individualistic terms as a personal relationship with God, freedom of religious conviction and the right to change religious affiliation tend to be given priority. This is typically the case with Protestant Christianity, which has been so much influenced by principles of the Western Enlightenment. A quite different worldview pertains among those churches that are historically rooted in the cultural and intellectual traditions of West Asia / North Africa, where community provides the social and spiritual context within which individual faith is nurtured. This is at the heart of the monastic tradition of Christianity and is inherent in the shape and content of the liturgy. In different ways it is no less evident in the Islamic religious consciousness, which has influenced the social character of indigenous Christianity. Evangelism in this context is understood in terms of the renewal of an individual's ecclesial identity within his or her denominational identity, not in separation from it. Orthodox witness makes this very clear and amounts to a conceptual (and thus practical) resistance to the many Western notions of mission.

Christian cultural identity in West Asia / North Africa. The intricate relationship between language and culture is richly evidenced in the indigenous Christian communities in West Asia / North Africa. Our review of the churches has emphasized the diversity of linguistic cultures (Aramaic, Armenian, Coptic, and Syriac) that distinguished the ancient Eastern patriarchates from each other and from the West (Greek and Latin). With the rise and expansion of Islam from the seventh century, however, Arabic has become the lingua franca of most of the peoples of the region. The wealth of Christian theological writing from the mid-eighth century in Arabic as well as in their ethnic languages is a literary monument of their bilingual traditions. Sydney Griffith, a leading scholar of this genre of Christian literature, observes that Christians "actually adopted a way of presenting the traditional teachings of the church in an Arabic idiom conditioned by the Islamic frame of reference in the midst of which they lived."[52] Rarely have Western missions been sensitive to this achievement. Indeed, if recognized at all, it has usually been regarded with suspicion as an incipient paganism that must be expunged. The conversion of indigenous Christians to Western forms of Christianity has had the effect of deracinating them from their cultural-linguistic traditions, marking them out as "aliens at home"[53] and burdening them with the criticism of being cultural proselytes.

Christian political identity in West Asia / North Africa. Under the Ottoman Empire the Christian communities of West Asia / North Africa were recognized for legal and political purposes as millets—autonomous minorities within Muslim society, represented by their clerical hierarchies. For four hundred years (early sixteenth to early twentieth centuries) this was the juridical framework of George Sabra's sociological category of "denominational" identity. While the millet system has been formally abolished in the constitutions of the modern Arab states, it continues to exert informal influence in terms of political psychology and practice. This is strikingly evident in Lebanon, where a "confessional" system of public life guarantees (in theory) that each religious community in the state is represented proportionately to its size in relation to the other religious communities. While political leadership is exercised on constitutionally secular lines, confessionalism allows the religious hierarchies of both Christian and Muslim communities to continue to exert considerable influence behind the scenes, and openly if political life breaks down in civil or military disorder.

Against this background the antagonism of indigenous churches to proselytism has certain political resonance. This may be construed as a case of clerical hierarchies protecting their political influence from further erosion. But since this is how the political culture continues to operate, it can also be argued that a politically influential clergy is a positive asset for Christian minorities in societies that are themselves undergoing various forms of Islamic religious and social renewal. Burdened by a feeling of vulnerability, many Arab Christians look for the strengthening of their traditional institutions of leadership and feel politically undermined and endangered by proselytism.

Conclusion

This article has attempted to elucidate the controversial issue of proselytism in West Asia / North Africa in a dispassionate manner, based on historical evidence and contemporary documentation, analyzed from the point of view of the indigenous Christian communities. In conclusion, the author wishes to commend the statement of George Sabra that "ecumenism is simply incompatible with proselytism."[54] The weight of historical evidence shows that proselytism almost invariably becomes the dynamic of intra-Christian relations where disunity prevails among churches or sectarianism is fostered by exclusivist groups. Ultimately, it is evangelism itself that becomes the casualty of "sheepstealing" mission.

If the renewal of the church arises from the renewal of Christian witness, the qualitative wealth of Christian traditions in West Asia / North Africa (notwithstanding their quantitative decline) suggests that this region has an important role to play in the twenty-first century, as it did in the first. But this promise will be realized only to the degree that the churches of the future can regain the ecumenical fellowship of the early Christian centuries. Drawing once again from Sabra's sociological analysis, we can well support his hope that in a truly ecumenical situation "the evangelizers could aim at reviving . . . sociological Christians in and for their own (ecclesial) traditions."[55]

Notes

1. The author acknowledges indebtedness and expresses gratitude to Carolyn Sperl, coordinator of Reference and Interlibrary Loan Services, Hartford Seminary, for assistance in researching the disparate literature relevant to this study. The colonialist associations and geographic ambiguities of the term "Middle East" and its variant "Near East" call for the less prejudicial (albeit less elegant) terminology "West Asia / North Africa," which will be used throughout.

2. Recent introductory studies of these churches include Roland Roberson, *The Eastern Churches: A Brief Survey*, rev. 3d ed. (Rome: Pont. Institutum Studiorum Orientalium, 1990), which deals with the Oriental and Eastern Orthodox and with the Catholic churches of West Asia / North Africa and elsewhere (but excludes the Protestants); and Norman Homer, *Guide to Christian Churches in the Middle East: Present-day Christianity in the Middle East and North Africa* (Elkhart, Ind.: Mission Focus Press, 1989), which includes information on the Protestant churches as well as the Oriental and Eastern Orthodox and the Catholics. A briefer summary appears in David Teague, ed., *Turning a New Leaf: Protestant Missions and the Orthodox Churches of the Middle East*, 2d ed. (London: Interserve; Lynnwood, Wash.: Middle East Media, 1992). For a sociopolitical overview of these Christian communities, see Robert Betts, *Christians in the Arab East: A Political Study*, rev. ed. (Atlanta: John Knox Press, 1978). For the contemporary statement of an Arab Christian, see Mitri Raheb, *I Am a Palestinian Christian* (Minneapolis: Fortress Press, 1995). Standard scholarly reference works include Aziz Atiyah, *A History of Eastern Christianity* (London: Methuen, 1968); and A. J. Arberry, ed., *Religion in the Middle East: Three Religions in Concord and Conflict*, vol. 1 (Cambridge: Cambridge Univ. Press, 1969).

3. For the MECC's account of the churches of its region, see "Who Are the Christians of the Middle East?" *MECC Perspectives* (Limassol, 1986).

4. The preamble of the document reads: "After a discussion process started in December 1986, the Commission on Faith and Unity studied in its last meeting (July 1989), before the Fifth General Assembly, a third draft. It has agreed that it should be considered 'A Study Document' submitted to the Executive Committee of the MECC and to the Churches and made available to institutions, groups or individuals concerned."

5. MECC study document, paragraphs 6–11. For an elaboration of these defi-

nitions, see George Sabra, "Proselytism, Evangelisation and Ecumenism," *Theological Review: Near East School of Theology* 9, no. 2 (1988): 23–36.

6. MECC study document, paragraphs 13–14.

7. Ibid., paragraph 39.

8. Ibid., paragraphs 20–29.

9. King Tiridate's conversion to Christianity at the hands of St. Gregory the Illuminator in 301 predates the baptism of Emperor Constantine around 337.

10. In Armenian canon law the catholicosate has global authority over Armenians, in contrast to the patriarchate, which has only regional jurisdiction. The church comprises two patriarchates (Jerusalem and Constantinople), which are dependent upon the catholicosate of Etchmiadzin. In the fifteenth century a second catholicosate was created for the Armenian diaspora in Cilicia, Syria (modern-day Lebanon).

11. The name "Assyrian" reflects their claim to descend from the ancient people of Nineveh. Alternatively, they call themselves "Chaldean." In either case they reject their designation by other churches as Nestorian, after the fifth-century theologian Nestorius, whom the Council of Ephesus condemned for allegedly teaching Dyophysitism, the view that the person of Jesus Christ included two separate natures.

12. The doctrinal issue turned once again on the problem of defining the person of Jesus Christ. Was he of a single divine nature as the Orientals were alleged to have asserted (Monophysitism), or of two natures that were united without confusion, change, division, or separation as the Western Christians insisted (Chalcedonianism)?

13. The recovery of the theological output of these churches within Muslim societies and culture is the goal of important contemporary research, much of which has been pioneered by Samir Khalil. For a recent example of this in English, see Samir Khalil and Jorgen Nielsen, eds., *Christian Arabic Apologists During the Abbasid Period (750–1258)* (Leiden: E. J. Brill, 1994).

14. The Arabization of the episcopate and election of the first Arab patriarch at the end of the nineteenth century stands as one of the early milestones of Arab nationalism.

15. In fairness to the Roman position, it must be acknowledged that Rome viewed the Eastern-rite churches within the Catholic communion as symbols of the full communion with the Eastern and Oriental Orthodox churches that is yet to be achieved. They were provisional models of reunion, or as the Second Vatican Council stated: "All these directives of law are laid down in view of the present situation, until such time as the Catholic Church and the separated Eastern Churches come together into complete unity" ("Decree on Eastern Catholic Churches," in *The Documents of Vatican II*, ed. Walter Abbott [New York: Guild Press, 1966], p. 385).

16. Created by the Latin Crusaders after their conquest of Jerusalem in 1099, this patriarchate did not survive the end of the Latin Kingdom of Jerusalem but was reconstituted by the Vatican in 1847.

17. *Documents of Vatican II*, p. 373.

18. For example, see Theodore Zissis, "Uniatism: A Problem in the Dialogue Between Orthodox and Roman Catholics," *Greek Orthodox Theological Review* 35 (Spring 1990): 21–31.

19. For analyses of the history of nineteenth-century evangelical missionary theory and practice in West Asia by indigenous scholars, see Habib Badr, "Mission to 'Nominal Christians': The Policy and Practice of the American Board of Commissioners for Foreign Missions and Its Missionaries" (Ph.D. diss., Princeton Univ., 1922; UMI no. 9229015); and Wanis Semaan, *Aliens at Home: A Socio-Religious Analysis of the Protestant Church in Lebanon and Its Backgrounds* (Beirut: Librairie du Liban/Longman, 1986).

20. Badr, "Mission to 'Nominal Christians,'" pp. 164–65. Anderson's study of this issue is found in his *History of the Missions of the American Board of Commissioners for Foreign Missions to the Oriental Churches*, 2 vols. (Boston: Congregational Publishing Society, 1872).

21. For example, see Henry Jessup, *The Greek Church and Protestant Missions; or, Missions to the Oriental Churches* (Beirut and New York: Christian Literature Company, 1891).

22. A contemporary American missionary, Isaac Bird, was the first to write on this incident in his *Martyr of Lebanon* (Boston: American Tract Society, 1864). Rufus Anderson later wrote a chapter "The Martyr of Lebanon, Assaad Shidyak" (*History*, 1:52ff.).

23. Badr, "Mission to 'Nominal Christians,'" pp. 100–102; cf. Semaan, *Aliens at Home*, pp. 82–85. The missionary significance of the First Church in Hartford lay in its minister from 1818 to 1867, Joel Hawes, who played a leading role in the Second Great Awakening. Hawes was a friend and supporter of Rufus Anderson, as well as his traveling companion on an extended visit to West Asia in 1844. On Joel Hawes, see George Walker, *History of the First Church in Hartford, 1633–1883* (Hartford, Conn.: Brown & Gross, 1884).

24. Badr, "Mission to 'Nominal Christians,'" p. 254.

25. Ibid., p. 264.

26. Anderson, *History*, 1:47.

27. See Horner, *Guide to Christian Churches in the Middle East*, pp. 65–79, for a full list of Anglican and Protestant churches in West Asia / North Africa.

28. Ibid., p. 72.

29. Zissis, "Uniatism," p. 22. Defining uniatism as no more than "a method of proselytizing the East," Zissis argues that it is a "fraudulent union" that should be abolished, asking that "the Uniates . . . be incorporated in the Latin rite of Roman Catholicism."

30. *Documents of Vatican II*, p. 34 ("Dogmatic Constitution on the Church").

31. Summary of salient points in the Joint Commission's 1991 working document entitled "Uniatism as a Method of Union in the Past and the Present Call for Full Communion," published in *Journal of the Moscow Patriarchate* 10 (1991): 60–62. For an interpretation of this document by an Eastern-rite Catholic priest, see Joseph Loya, "Uniatism in Current Ecumenical Dia-

logue," *Ecumenical Trends: Graymoor Ecumenical and Interreligious Institute* 21, no. 6 (June 1992): 83–86.

32. Donald Wagner, *Anxious for Armageddon: A Call to Partnership for Middle Eastern and Western Christians* (Waterloo, Ont.; Scottdale, Pa.: Herald Press, 1994), pp. 181–82; see also 57–58 and 186–87. For a report on the 1991 Cyprus meeting, see Kim Lawton, "The Other Peace Conference: Middle Eastern and Western Christians Hold a Summit Meeting of Their Own to Resolve Long-standing Tensions," *Christianity Today*, November 11, 1991, pp. 46–48.

33. David Teague's phrase, which he uses as the title of the chapter in which he speaks of what he learned through personal encounter with Coptic Orthodoxy in Egypt (*Turning Over a New Leaf*, pp. 63–84).

34. Wagner, *Anxious for Armageddon*, pp. 181, 96–113.

35. This often-cited quotation appears, for example, in Ion Bria, ed., *Martyria/Mission: The Witness of the Orthodox Church* (Geneva: WCC Commission on World Mission and Evangelism, 1980), pp. 66–67; see also Ion Bria, ed., *Go Forth in Peace: Orthodox Perspectives on Mission* (Geneva: WCC Mission Series, 1986), p. 38.

36. Bria, *Martyria/Mission*, p. 68.

37. Ibid., p. 226.

38. Ibid., p. 10.

39. Ibid., p. 228.

40. On the role of monastic witness in Orthodoxy, see ibid. pp. 243–48.

41. Ibid., p. 230.

42. Case studies of cross-cultural witness appear in George Lemopoulos, ed., *Your Will Be Done: Orthodoxy in Mission* (Geneva: WCC Commission on World Mission and Evangelism, 1989).

43. For a sociohistorical analysis, see Robert Haddad, *Syrian Christians in Muslim Society* (Princeton: Princeton Univ. Press, 1970). For a more theological perspective, see N. M. Vaporis, ed., *Orthodox Christians and Muslims* (Brookline, Mass.: Holy Cross Orthodox Press, 1986).

44. "Witnessing in the Islamic Context," in *Your Will Be Done*, ed. Lemopoulos, pp. 95–104, from which the following quotations are taken.

45. For further information, see Milia Khouri, "The Mission of the Orthodox Youth in Lebanon," in *Your Will Be Done*, ed. Lemopoulos, pp. 181–83.

46. Qur'an 5:15: "For those, too, who call themselves Christians, We did take a Covenant, but they forgot a good part of the Message that We sent them. So We estranged them, with enmity and hatred between one and another, to the Day of Judgment. And soon will God show them what they have done" (Yusuf Ali, *The Holy Qur'an: Text, Translation, and Commentary*, pp. 245–46).

47. The leading contemporary Orthodox theologian to have addressed the issue of the Christian relationship to Islam is Metropolitan Georges Khodr of Lebanon; see his "Christianity in a Pluralistic World: The Economy of the Holy Spirit," *Ecumenical Review* 23 (April 1971): 118–28. For a discussion of

the contextualization of Christian theology, including Orthodox contributions, in Palestinian Muslim society, see Andre Mazawi, "Palestinian Local Theology and the Issue of Islamo-Christian Dialogue: An Appraisal," *Islamochristiana* 19 (1993): 93–115.

48. MECC study document, paragraphs 34–37.

49. The phrase is used by the former MECC general secretary Gabriel Habib in his letter to evangelicals, "Renewal, Unity, and Witness in the Middle East:. An Open Letter to Evangelicals," *Evangelical Missions Quarterly* 26 (July 1990): 256–62. See also Michael Roemmele's reply in the same issue, pp. 260–62.

50. MECC study document, paragraphs 61–64. On this point, George Sabra argues that an appeal to secular authorities, or to the courts other than in cases where proselytizing groups breach national laws, infringes the religious rights of individuals, denies the spirit of the Gospel, and betrays the witness of the earliest Christians, who courageously stood for freedom of faith against the political, legal, military, and social pressures of the Roman Empire ("Proselytism, Evangelization, and Ecumenism," pp. 26–28).

51. Sabra, "Proselytism, Evangelization, and Ecumenism," pp. 29–31.

52. Sydney Griffith, "Faith and Reason in Christian Kalam: Theodore Abu Qurrah on Discerning the True Religion," in *Christian Arabic Apologists During the Abbasid Period (750–1258),* ed. Khalil and Nielsen, p. 5.

53. See Semaan, *Aliens at Home,* a socioreligious study of the evangelical church in Lebanon.

54. Sabra, "Proselytism, Evangelization, and Ecumenism," p. 25.

55. Ibid., p. 33.

9

Prepositions and Salvation

Kenneth Cragg

There is an old, well-worn story of a stranger in Ireland asking a local worthy for direction concerning "the way to Roscommon." He got the laconic reply: "If I were going to Roscommon, I would not be starting from here."

Christian converse about "interfaith," as in Richard J. Jones's article in the July 1992 issue of the INTERNATIONAL BULLETIN OF MISSIONARY RESEARCH, "Islam as a Way of Salvation," frequently assumes that "salvation" is the right, the agreed, and the proper denominator from which to start. Yet it begs many questions. For "salvation" is such an elusive term, and even if the parties accept it (probably in deference to *our* starting point), it connotes quite contrasted things. Nor does it greatly help to distinguish "cosmic" from "mundane," especially so if the former entails the further decision about "damnation" and whether and by whom it is incurred. Encounters have for too long been too much preoccupied with "Are there few that be saved?" and which "few" may they be?

Salvation *in, for, by, of, from*—the implications bewilder when we begin to think about the prepositions without which the word is vacant. Richard Jones reports Wilfred Cantwell Smith as holding that "to have faith is to be saved," and that "saving faith" is present in the very recognition of the "ought," even if the sense of obligation remains unfulfilled in concrete acts.

The rugged Epistle of James has a different view. To be sure, Wilfred Smith sees "faith" as always a singular noun quite distinct from "traditional beliefs" through which its essential quality of "humane transcendent awareness" may be diversely expressed. In that way we could use "faith" as a verb and speak of "faithing" just as we speak of "hoping." Then "faithing" is the name of a universal human experience of ultimacy and obligation, in the sense that we should never speak of "other faiths" but only of "other folk." We could then perhaps coin "salvationed" and use it comparably of all participants in "faith."

Wilfred Smith's instinct to focus issues into terms is always salutary. Yet are the prescripts too sanguine, too intellectual? What if some in our time have contrived to live effectively without any transcendental awareness? Is faith really a universal experience? Or what are we to make of the forms of it that are too evident in zealotry, bigotry, assertiveness, and hardness of heart? Is everything that is "religious" thereby either admirable or desirable? If ugly manifestations are seen as emanating sinfully from a set of beliefs, and if "faith" is the language of which these are the grammars, what ought we to conclude about "salvation"? Do some believers stultify their faith by the very means in which they give it form?

It would seem that there has to be some transforming, revolutionary dimension to "salvation," a crisis element by which the self-question that is at the heart of it may be resolved. And let us not simply pose that self-question in terms of eternal destiny. There is more than enough to occupy it here and now. All that may be subsequent to time must be in the hands of the Eternal.

For the Theravadin in Theravada Buddhism, the jailer's question at the Philippian prison, "What must I do to be saved?" is setting individuality at the heart of yearning, when the true wisdom is that salvation comes only in seeing through the illusion of both individuality and yearning. To imagine a persona that might be "saved," and to think of this as "eternal life" for some immortal "me," is to start from where one can never arrive. "Salvation" from this perspective is *not* some remade "self" but an unmade "self" in the quest not for "extinction" (since there is essentially no-thing to extinguish) but for the attainment of "not-being" through *dukkha* to *anatta* through a register of inclusive transience into the bliss, at length, of the "desired undesiring."

If we want to use the odd word "salvific," it is clear that "salvifics" do not tally: indeed, they are totally at odds.

Not all moods of Buddhism, nor the diversities of Hinduism, are so decisive about "undesiring." Some struggle heroically, as does Raimundo Panikkar in his many writings, somehow to reconcile *bhakti* devotion to a personal "Lord" from a significant selfhood with the "oceanic feeling" of totally abated being, where "Thou" and "I" no longer have meaning. It would seem impossible to comprehend under the single term "salvation" such different readings of what can be saved and how and whence and whither. We can grasp the *anatta*, "nonself," concept by analogy with what Paul writes about idol meats and the "weaker brother." Truly the idol is a nonentity, and therefore all meats are clean. The free mind has no need to defer to notions that have no reality. Yet, for the weaker brother in his illusion idols are all too real and—given their reality—he must assume that the apostle is party to their acknowledgment. Therefore Paul will abstain from idol meats in deference to the deluded brethren until they can be undeluded. In respect of imagined selfhood, we are the "weaker ones" who proceed upon illusion. When we have become undeluded, we will cease to ask for a salvation, or rather we will be finding it only in surrender of our search.

The Semitic monotheisms are not caught in this situation, since they all proceed upon the essential clue of the "me-ness" of us all—its creaturehood, authenticity, responsibility, vocation, and destiny. "O God, thou art my God"; "The Lord is my shepherd"; "When you said to me: Seek ye my face, my heart said to you: Your face, Lord, will I seek."

Yet that divine/human situation is diversely comprehended by synagogue, church, and mosque. Judaism and Islam dispense with Christology-within-theology. Leo Baeck used to insist that "in Judaism there are no retailers of salvation." Ismail al-Faruqi coined the terms "peccatism" and "saviorism" to decry a theology of redemption. Both Judaism and Islam are text-oriented faiths assuming a human adequacy and competence to achieve a due order of life independent of divine intervention and "grace." Where their experiences seem to belie their assurance, the appeal must be to await a future when a true Sabbath will be truly kept and when Islam will be truly Islam.

There are, of course, vast questions here for the Christian measure of "salvation," necessitated by the radical Christian realism about our human capacity for wrong and our perversity over against law, and necessitated also as larger demands upon the resources of divine sovereignty and magnanimity. At the heart of Christian "salvation" is a divine kenosis, a redemptive self-expenditure of a God "who does not economize himself" but in shepherd character seeks and finds and saves. What is more unstinted in the divine responds to what is more necessitous in the human. Christian "salvation" locates itself in a representative encounter between what we can identify as "the sin of the world" and a suffering love that we can duly relate to the eternal mind. The place is the cross, where we come to God through and because of Jesus—this teacher, this master, this Christ—only because, as the event constrains us to believe, God is "come to" in him.

The "neither is there salvation in any other," however, is not some rigorous cornering of the means of grace, some perquisite of sole proprietors. It is eminently reproducible in "Christ-bearers" (not "anonymous Christians") who are ready to read the world as the arena of the love that suffers and join themselves with the forgivingness of Christ in every place. Yet that quality of "savingness" will always need the paradigm of the event to which the church witnesses, where warrant may be found for the risk in such a saving faith. That "God is Christ" cannot be proved, it can be trusted. At a bitter point in her often bitter quest, Virginia Woolf asked: "Why is there not a discovery in life: something one can lay hands on and say: 'This is it'?"

One way of identifying "salvation" is just such a discovery, a "This is it!" Faith can say this about this someone and this somehow meeting us, like food to hunger and love to its welcome. Only by the way it includes us might it be thought to be exclusive.

10

Missiometrics 2006: Goals, Resources, Doctrines of the 350 Christian World Communions

David B. Barrett, Todd M. Johnson, and Peter F. Crossing

Global Table 1. Christian workers in the context of global Christianity and its mission, with comparison with other large religions.

The problem raised by most varieties of statistics of workers is that the world's 37,000 denominations count and publish their annual figures with their own definitions of categories which differ from most other denominations' usage. This means that each's figures cannot be simply added to get global totals. For example, 'retired' clergy continue to preach, visit, and serve in local churches after their retirement; others, though officially retired, continue to write major books or work in broadcasting. Thousands of independent workers function with no organizational ties.

The next Paragraph enumerates the global context in 2007; next, Paragraphs A, B, C, and D enumerate for 2005 a selection of the more significant varieties of Christian workers, with overall totals in A = B + C + D, followed by a sampling of lesser categories. Statistics in Global Tables 2 to 4 relate mainly to 2005. Paragraph D on this page as the major mission category is set in bold type. Lastly, Paragraph E enumerates non-Christian workers.

Global status of Christianity in AD 2007 (65.8 generations after Christ): of world population of 6,616 millions (55% female), 66.8% (4.4 billions) are non-Christians (49% female), 33.2% (2,196 millions) are Christians (44.0% of them being White, 56.0% Non-White), of whom 31.4% (2,078 millions) are affiliated church members in 350 Christian World Communions, 10.6% (703,225,000, up from 688,000,000 in 2005) are Great Commission Christians committed to Christ's worldwide mission, including 258,669,000 Evangelicals and 602,792,000 Renewalists (Pentecostals, Charismatics, Neocharismatics); of the wider world, 72.0%

(4,765 millions) are evangelized (aware of the Gospel), with Scriptures directly translated into 2,238 languages (424 with whole Bible, 1,000 with New Testament only, and 814 with a gospel only), or Scriptures indirectly available in 7,364 languages (2,256 with Bible or near-Bible, 3,228 with NT or near-NT, and 1,880 with a Portion or near-Portion).

A. *Total all full-time Christian workers*: 11,525,000 (61% men 7,085,000, 39% women 4,440,000), consisting of 1.2 million ordained male clergy/priests/pastors/ministers/deacons/preachers, 500,000 ordained women, 3,440,000 religious personnel (in 2,500 religious orders, institutes, and congregations), 300,000 ordained brothers, 6,385,000 lay workers, 348,000 lay missionaries (so designated), 500,000 monks, 50,000 friars, 1,490,000 nuns, 1.1 million sisters, 3,506,000 catechists, 71,000 colporteurs, 35,000 bishops/presidents/moderators/metropolitans/patriarchs, 800,000 evangelists/teachers, 360,000 administrators, 330,000 accountants, 410,000 short-term missionaries, 6,000 nonresidential missionaries, 1,052,000 theologians, 32,000 missiologists, 1.0 million seminarians (in 5,000 seminaries); retired workers 116,000, of whom 81,000 are pensioned and 35,000 unpensioned.

B. *Christian home pastoral workers* (those not usually regarded or termed as missionaries): 5,012,000 (47% men, 53% women), 1,090,000 clergy (290,000 being women), religious personnel 2,585,000 (26% men, 74% women), lay personnel 1,337,000, seminarians 650,000. Also a large number of men and of women work as missionaries of regular mission agencies, unknown to the churches because they function completely independently.

C. *Christian home mission personnel* (home missionaries, defined as all workers who are citizens of the country they work in, and are usually recognized and termed as missionaries): 6,070,000 (74% men, 26% women); mostly related to the world's 37,000 denominations; 480,000 clergy/priests/pastors/ ministers/deacons, including preachers, lay preachers, radio/TV preachers, 100 mega-evangelists, evangelizers, chaplains, lay readers, missioners, mission partners, 3,500,000 catechists, 60,000 colporteurs, 590,000 local evangelists/teachers; 120,000 administrators, 130,000 accountants; most personnel use e-mail online, in 2,000 languages; incapacitated or sick workers, 44,000; retired home missionaries 56,000, of whom 16,000 remain unpensioned; background supporters in mission (Great Commission Christians) 220 million.

D. *Christian foreign mission personnel* (foreign missionaries, defined as all workers who are aliens (noncitizens) in the country they work in): **443,000 in 4,340 mission-sending agencies (55% men, 45% women; 80% abroad at any one time, 20% absent on home leave): 100,000 male clergy/ ministers, 30,000 ordained women; 120,000 male lay workers, 98,000 women lay workers; 135,000 married men, 110,000 unmarried men (singles, widowers, celibates, monks, contemplatives, friars); 95,000 married women (homemakers, wives, widows), 103,000 unmarried women (23,000 singles, 50,000 nuns, 20,000 sisters); traditional categories of worker – pastoral, medical, educational, agricultural, also broadcasters, scripture translators and distributors; 130,000 are career missionaries (over 10 years of service abroad); missionaries using e-mail online 410,000 in 5,000 languages; 8,000 independent missionaries (unaffiliated to any agency); missionaries murdered, 130 a year; incapacitated or sick missionaries 4,000; missionaries' children (under 15s) 31,000; professional tentmakers 210,000, short-termers (under 1 year abroad) 410,000; 210,000 ex foreign missionaries (prematurely resigning) in attrition rate of 12,000 per year; retired foreign missionaries 10,000, of whom 3,000 remain unpensioned; background supporters in mission (Great Commission Christians) 468 million.**

E. *Non-Christian foreign missionaries sent abroad*: Muslims (who number 20.4% of the world) send out 200,000 engaging in Dawah (missionary activity) in 60 countries; Hindus and Neo-Hindus (13.5% of the world) send out 20,000; Buddhists (5.9% of the world) send out 20,000; Baha'is, Chinese universists, Sikhs, Jews, and Neoreligionists all send out significant numbers; with a grand total for all non-Christians (who number 66.9% of the world) sending out some 300,000 workers to 210 foreign countries.

Global Table 2. **Varieties and totals of the world's full-time Christian pastoral and mission personnel AD 2005.**

COLUMNS. *Full-time ecclesiastical workers/personnel are here shown in 4 large columns: A, B, C, and D, where D = Foreign mission, C = Home mission, B = Home pastoral work (non-missionary), and A = global total = B + C + D. Each of the 4 columns is then subdivided by gender into Men, and Women.* **ROWS.** *Each of the 39 rows of data that follow refers to its global category and global totals. Related personnel are categorized by 8 major varieties shown in capitals on Rows 1, 3, 10, 12, 18, 26, 38, and 41. Category totals (Rows 2, 4, 10, 12, 18, 26, 38, and 41) are shown in bold type. Under these 8 some 39 ecclesiastical categories are then listed and enumerated. All numbers are given to the nearest thousand to allow for minor overlaps and differing definitions among Christianity's 37,000 denominations and its 350 Christian World Communions. Definitions of all rows are given on pages 136 and 137.*

Row	Column	1	2	3	4	5	6	7	8
		A. ALL WORKERS		B. HOME PASTORAL		C. HOME MISSION		D. FOREIGN MISSION	
		11,525,000		5,012,000		6,070,000		443,000	
	SPHERE OF WORK								
1.	Total all workers								
3.	GENDER	Men	Women	Men	Women	Men	Women	Men	Women
4.	Total workers by gender	7,085,000	4,440,000	2,360,000	2,652,000	4,480,000	1,590,000	245,000	198,000
5.	Gender, %	61	39	47	53	74	26	55	45
6.	Married	5,585,000	1,482,000	1,820,000	587,000	3,630,000	800,000	135,000	95,000
7.	Unmarried	1,500,000	2,958,000	540,000	2,065,000	850,000	790,000	110,000	103,000
8.	Singles	620,000	418,000	260,000	165,000	300,000	230,000	60,000	23,000
9.	Celibates	880,000	2,540,000	280,000	1,900,000	550,000	560,000	50,000	80,000
10.	CLERGY	1,200,000	500,000	800,000	290,000	300,000	180,000	100,000	30,000
11.	Bishops	30,000	5,000	20,000	2,000	5,000	1,000	5,000	2,000
12.	RELIGIOUS personnel	850,000	2,590,000	685,000	1,900,000	140,000	620,000	25,000	70,000
13.	Monks	500,000	—	455,000	—	40,000	—	5,000	—
14.	Friars	50,000	—	30,000	—	10,000	—	10,000	—
15.	Brothers	300,000	—	200,000	—	90,000	—	10,000	—
16.	Nuns	—	1,490,000	—	1,000,000	—	440,000	—	50,000
17.	Sisters	—	1,100,000	—	900,000	—	180,000	—	20,000
18.	LAY personnel	5,035,000	1,350,000	875,000	462,000	4,040,000	790,000	120,000	98,000
19.	Lay missionaries	200,000	148,000	90,000	50,000	90,000	40,000	20,000	58,000
20.	Lay ministers	700,000	270,000	470,000	150,000	200,000	100,000	30,000	20,000
21.	Catechists	3,005,000	501,000	—	—	3,000,000	500,000	5,000	1,000
22.	Colporteurs	60,000	11,000	—	—	50,000	10,000	10,000	1,000
23.	Evangelists/Teachers	600,000	195,000	100,000	80,000	480,000	110,000	20,000	5,000
24.	Administrators	250,000	110,000	118,000	79,000	100,000	20,000	32,000	11,000
25.	Accountants	220,000	115,000	97,000	103,000	120,000	10,000	3,000	2,000
26.	AUXILIARY personnel	1,924,000	326,000	1,450,000	238,000	354,000	36,000	120,000	52,000
27.	Furloughed/On leave	47,000	36,000	25,000	24,000	10,000	5,000	12,000	7,000
28.	Sick/ill personnel	52,000	31,000	20,000	15,000	30,000	14,000	2,000	2,000
29.	Short-term missionaries	260,000	150,000	—	—	—	—	260,000	150,000
30.	Nonresidential missionaries	5,000	1,000	—	—	—	—	5,000	1,000
31.	Pilgrim evangelizers	50,000	50,000	—	—	—	—	50,000	50,000
32.	Tourist evangelizers	150,000	350,000	—	—	—	—	150,000	350,000
33.	Tent-makers	180,000	30,000	—	—	—	—	180,000	30,000
34.	Seminarians	800,000	200,000	500,000	150,000	200,000	10,000	100,000	40,000
35.	Theologians	1,000,000	52,000	900,000	45,000	96,000	5,000	4,000	2,000
36.	Missiologists	25,000	7,000	5,000	4,000	18,000	2,000	2,000	1,000
37.	Ex foreign missionaries	90,000	120,000	—	—	—	—	90,000	120,000
38.	RETIRED personnel	75,000	41,000	30,000	20,000	40,000	16,000	5,000	5,000
39.	Pensioned	52,000	29,000	18,000	16,000	30,000	10,000	4,000	3,000
40.	Unpensioned	23,000	12,000	12,000	4,000	10,000	6,000	1,000	2,000
41.	BACKGROUND supporters	300 million	388 million	—	—	90 million	130 million	210 million	258 million

DEFINITIONS OF ROWS in Global Table 2.

1. **SPHERE OF WORK.** Description by the 4 categories of sphere of work: A, B, C, and D, and by the 7 varieties of personnel shown below as Rows in bold type.
2. Total all global workers combined (men and women), for all categories, in AD 2005. This total for each column = A = B + C + D, also for Rows 10 + 12 + 18. Note: in this table, 'mission personnel' involves only Rows 2 to 25, and is strictly defined as in Rows 10 + 12 + 18 (sometimes termed 'career missionaries').
3. **GENDER** (Rows 3 to 9): Men, Women for each variety. Note in several areas of Christian work, spouses do not call themselves workers unless specifically and officially so designated.
4. Total workers by gender: Men, Women. Note expansion of foreign mission personnel by gender: AD 1800, 25,000 (20,000 men, 5,000 women); AD 1900, 62,000 (47,000 men, 15,000 women); AD 1970, 240,000 (144,000 men, 96,000 women); AD 2005, as shown in Row 4.
5. Total workers by gender, % for each column (column 4 divided by column 2 times 100).
6. Workers married (omitting the many spouses of Christian workers who do not consider themselves also as Christian workers or mission personnel).
7. Workers unmarried.
8. Singles (unmarried, no vows).
9. Celibates (vows): those who have taken vows of celibacy or poverty.
10. **CLERGY (clerical personnel):** Ordained ministers/priests/pastors/deacons/preachers/chaplains/missioners, including Row 11.
11. Bishops/moderators/presidents, metropolitans, patriarchs, primates, popes (counted also in Row 10).
12. **RELIGIOUS personnel:** (members of religious orders, congregations or institutes (= Rows 12 to 17) excluding clergy (already enumerated here under Row 10)).
13. Monks (contemplatives, usually in the 9,000 monasteries).
14. Friars (mendicants, including OFM, OP).
15. Brothers (vows), usually in organized orders or agencies.
16. Nuns (strict vows, contemplatives).
17. Sisters (simple vows, serving outside convents).
18. **LAITY, LAY personnel** (= Rows 18 to 25).
19. Lay missionaries (so designated).
20. Lay ministers (unordained but serving temporarily or permanently as ministers).
21. Catechists (serving in their home countries alongside foreign missionaries).

22. Colporteurs (itinerant Bible sales and Scripture distribution personnel).
23. Evangelists/Teachers (church teachers in own countries); including itinerant evangelists.
24. Administrators, to administer personnel and support at home or abroad.
25. Accountants, treasurers, responsible for handling churches' total income of US$360 billion per annum (see Global Table 5, Rows 58-60).
26. **AUXILIARY personnel:** (Rows 26 to 37 are noted here but not counted in Rows 3 to 25; likewise with Rows 38 to 40).
27. Furloughed/ On home leave (or otherwise absent from their primary work area); average time of foreign service 5 years.
28. Sick/ill personnel temporarily inactive in long-term situations.
29. Short-term missionaries (serving abroad, from 2 weeks to under one year).
30. Nonresidential foreign missionaries working with an unevangelized people in an unreached (World A) country but domiciled in their own country or a different one, with unrestricted communications and freedom of ministry.
31. Pilgrim evangelizers: pilgrims to a Christian shrine in a foreign unreached area, deliberately as evangelizers.
32. Tourist evangelizers: Christian individuals, families, churches, denominations touring a World A foreign country, deliberately as evangelizers.
33. Tent-makers (in secular posts abroad but assisting foreign missionaries in their work).
34. Seminarians (enrolled theological students usually working towards ordination).
35. Theologians, Bible teachers (duplication, since also counted in Rows 10, 12, 18).
36. Missiologists (duplication).
37. Ex foreign missionaries: formerly employed by a church or mission agency, then resigned prematurely and took other employment. This rate of missionary attrition averages 5% per year or 50% per decade.
38. **RETIRED personnel** (for workers in Rows 10 + 12 + 18 only), usually over 60 or 65 years old.
39. Pensioned (retirees whose former employer provides old-age pension obligation).
40. Unpensioned (workers who reach retirement age and then discover their former employer has no retirement or old-age pension plans).
41. **BACKGROUND supporters** of Christian mission (also termed Great Commission Christians, active on behalf of Christ's world mission but not enrolled as employed church workers in Rows 10, 12, 18).

Global Table 3. **Foreign mission personnel sent out across the world via 350 Christian World Communions.**

A Christian World Communion (CWC) is defined as an ongoing body uniting only churches and denominations with one similar ecclesiastical tradition or characteristic ('Adventist', 'Anglican', 'Baptist', 'Ecumenical', 'Evangelical', 'Lutheran', 'Mennonite', 'Methodist', 'Orthodox', 'Pentecostal', 'Reformed', 'Roman Catholic', etc.).

Meaning of 5 columns
1. *Involvement of each CWC ranked by categories 1 to 10 (attitude to either ecumenical or non-ecumenical confessionalism as explained in the 10 first lines across each list of titles)*
2. *Each CWC's official title (in English, with vernacular titles added only where necessary to establish identity)*
3. *Each CWC's affiliated church members*
4-5. *Each CWC's personnel, in 2 descriptive letters*
4. *External strength: each CWC's foreign mission personnel sent out, coded A to E as follows:*
    A = Massive strength, over 100,000 personnel
    B = Major strength, from 30,000 to 100,000 personnel
    C = Moderate strength, from 10,000 to 30,000 personnel
    D = Minor strength, from 1,000 to 10,000 personnel
    E = Minimal strength, under 1,000 personnel
5. *Internal influence on members: foreign mission personnel per million members, coded a to e as follows:*
    a = massive influence, over 250 personnel per million
    b = major influence, from 100 to 250 personnel per million
    c = moderate influence, from 50 to 100 personnel per million
    d = minor influence, from 20 to 50 personnel per million
    e = minimal influence, under 20 personnel per million

1	2	3	4,5
Involvement	*CWC Title*	*Members*	*Pers*
1. Conference of Secretaries of Christian World Communions (CSCWC), 1957-2006			
Anglican Consultative Council (ACC)/Anglican Communion		79,739,000	Cb
Baptist World Alliance (BWA)		101,000,000	Dc
Church of the Brethren (German Pietists/Dunkers)		346,000	Eb
Disciples Ecumenical Committee for Consultation (DECC)		1,500,000	Ec
Ecumenical Patriarchate of Constantinople		17,594,000	Ec
Friends World Committee for Consultation (FWCC)		507,000	Eb
General Conference of Seventh-day Adventists (SDA)		25,000,000	Ca
International Moravian Church in Unity of Brethren		1,042,000	Ec
International Old Catholic Bishops Conference (IOCBC)		910,000	Ec
Lutheran World Federation (LWF)		80,000,000	Ca

1	2	3	4,5
Involvement	*CWC Title*	*Members*	*Pers*
Mennonite World Conference (MWC)		2,883,000	Eb
Orthodox Patriarchate of Moscow		111,404,000	Dd
Pentecostal World Fellowship (PWF)		29,821,000	Db
Reformed Ecumenical Council (REC)		7,347,000	Ee
Roman Catholic Church (RCC) (13 Patriarchates)		1,129,685,000	Aa
Salvation Army (SA)		2,214,000	Ea
World Alliance of Reformed Churches (WARC)		70,000,000	Cb
World Convention of Churches of Christ (WCCC)		10,000,000	Da
World Council of Churches (WCC/COE/ORK)		486,000,000	Bb
World Evangelical Alliance (WEA)		420,000,000	Aa
World Methodist Council (WMC)		70,226,000	Db

2. Not in CSCWC directly but related through a member participant

Bulgarian Orthodox Patriarchate of Sofia		11,769,000	Ee
Catholic Charismatic Renewal (CCR, ICCRS)		120,000,000	Ba
Council of Catholic Patriarchs in the East (10 Patriarchates)		5,400,000	Ee
Global Forum of Christian Churches & Ecumenical Organizations		200,000,000	Dd
Greek Orthodox Patriarchate of Alexandria		889,000	Eb
Greek Orthodox Patriarchate of Antioch		1,026,000	Eb
Greek Orthodox Patriarchate of Jerusalem		115,000	Ed
International Pentecostal Holiness Church (IPHC)		1,052,000	Eb
Orthodox Apostolic Catholicate of Georgia		2,536,000	Ed
Romanian Orthodox Patriarchate of Bucharest		19,780,000	Ed
Sacred Congregation for Bishops (3 Patriarchates)		884,875,000	Cd
Sacred Congregation for the Evangelization of Peoples (SCEP)		220,304,000	Aa
Sacred Congregation for the Oriental Churches (6 Patriarchal Synods)		15,312,000	Ed
Serbian Orthodox Patriarchate of Belgrade		7,642,000	Ed
Synod of Bishops (Synodus Episcoporum)		300,000,000	Bb
Waldensian Evangelical Church		54,000	Ea

3. WCC-related bodies not members of CSCWC because never invited

Ancient Assyrian Patriarchate of the East		500,000	Ec
Armenian Apostolic Catholicossate of Cilicia		852,000	Ea
Armenian Apostolic Patriarchate of Constantinople		66,000	Ea
Armenian Apostolic Patriarchate of Echmiadzin		5,593,000	Ed
Armenian Apostolic Patriarchate of Jerusalem		18,100	Ea
Brazil for Christ Evangelical Pentecostal Church (OBPC)		2,000,000	Ee
Consultation on Uniting and United Churches (CUUC)		54,205,000	Dc
Coptic Orthodox Patriarchate of Alexandria		10,354,000	Ee
Czechoslovak Hussite Church (CCH/CHC)		221,000	Eb
Eritrean Orthodox Patriarchate of Asmara		1,904,000	Ed
Ethiopian Orthodox Patriarchate of Addis Ababa		26,093,000	Ee
Great and Holy Council of the Orthodox Church (9 Patriarchates)		185,000,000	Dc
International Charismatic Consultation on World Evangelization		5,100,000	Ed
Mar Thoma Syrian Church of Malabar		1,115,000	Ec
Organization of African Instituted Churches (OAIC)		33,002,000	Db

1	2	3	4,5
Involvement	*CWC Title*	*Members*	*Pers*
	Oriental Orthodox Churches Conference (10 Patriarchates)	49,974,000	Dd
	Orthodox Syrian Catholicate of the East (OSCE)	2,575,000	Ed
	Philippine Independent Church (IFI/PIC)	3,425,000	Ed
	Syriac Orthodox Catholicossate of India	1,300,000	Ed
	Universal Syriac Orthodox Patriarchate of Antioch	1,219,000	Eb

4. Monoconfessional Anglican minicommunions

Anglican Communion Network (ACN)		1,000,000	Ec
International Communion of the Charismatic Episcopal Church (ICCEC)		950,000	Ea
Traditional Anglican Communion (TAC)		400,000	Eb

16 other schismatic communions ex Anglicanism/Episcopalianism,
including: Anglican Church International Communion, Anglican Orthodox
Communion (AOC), Communion of the Evangelical Episcopal
Church (CEEC), Reformed Episcopal Church (REC), et alia   7,600,000   Ec

5. African/Amerindian/Asian/Black/Latino/Oceanic minicommunions

Catholic Apostolic Church of Brazil.(ICAB)	3,000,000	Ee
Celestial Church of Christ (CCC/ECC)	4,436,000	Db
Christian Congregation of Brazil (Congregação Crista do Brasil)	3,120,000	Ea
Church of Christ/Iglesia ni Cristo (Manalista)	4,324,000	Ec
Church of God in Christ (CoGiC)	10,000,000	Da
Church of Jesus Christ through Simon Kimbangu (Eglise Kimbanguiste)	8,990,000	Eb
Cornerstone Gospel Church (Igreja Pedra Fundamental, IPF)	3,200,000	Eb
Deeper Life Bible Church (DLBC)	9,000,000	Da
Indian Pentecostal Church of God (IPCG)	977,000	Eb
International Evangelical Gypsy Social Association (ASNITE)	390,000	Eb
Jesus is Lord Fellowship (JILF)	2,277,000	Eb
Pentecostal Methodist Church of Chile (IMPC)	720,000	Eb
Universal Church of the Kingdom of God (UCKG/IURD)	5,431,000	Eb
Zion Christian Church (ZCC)	9,100,000	Ec

50 other Neocharismatic or Independent Non-White minicommunions each with
under a million members worldwide who maintain or function as a separate
communion: AACJM,AIPCA,CGMI,IFDA,IPDA,NMBCA, et alia   40,000,000   Db

6. European/North American monodenominational Protestant minicommunions

70 major Protestant global denominations each linked with its worldwide
daughter churches to form a separate communion: AEF, AIM, ARPC, AWM,
CAM, CBI, Christian Brethren (CMML), EPC, LAM, OD, OM, OMF, OMS,
SBC(IMB), SIM, TEAM, WEC, Worldwide Church of God (WCG), et alia   42,084,000   Ca

7. White-led Neocharismatic communions uninterested in CSCWC

Chaplaincy of Full Gospel Churches (CFGC)	8,385,000	Ec
Coalition of Spirit-filled Churches (CSC)	500,000	Ec
International Communion of Charismatic Churches (ICCC)	6,000,000	Ec
International Fellowship of Charismatic Churches (IFCC)	2,000,000	Ec
Manna Church International (Mana Igreja Crista)	200,000	Ea

1	*2*	*3*	*4,5*
Involvement	*CWC Title*	*Members*	*Pers*
Morning Star International		1,100,000	Da
Union of Messianic Jewish Congregations (UMJC)		142,000	Ec
Willow Creek Association of Churches (WCAC)		804,000	Ea
30 other White-led Neo-Apostolic meganetworks each globally			
>50,000, plus a handful of smaller but significant bodies: AFMA,			
AIMS, EFICC, ICF, SACOC, UICC, YWAM, et alia		50,815,000	Db

8. Conservative communions opposed to ecumenism, to WCC, to CSCWC

Alliance World Fellowship (AWF)	4,366,000	Da
Apostolic World Christian Fellowship (AWCF)	6,639,000	Ed
Assembly Hall Churches (Local Churches, Little Flock)	2,323,000	Da
Baptist Bible Fellowship International (BBFI)	2,500,000	Ea
Christian Holiness Association (CHA)	5,000,000	Ec
Global Network of Mission Structures (GNMS)	24,000,000	Db
International Conference of Reformed Churches (ICRC)	132,000	Ec
International Federation of Free Evangelical Churches (IFFEC)	846,000	Ed
International Lutheran Council (ILC)	3,546,000	Eb
International Spiritual Baptist Ministerial Council	20,000	Ec
New Apostolic Church (Neuapostolische Kirche: NAC/NAK)	11,098,000	Da
Old Ritualist Churches (Old Believers, Old Orthodox)	1,899,000	Ed
True Jesus Church (TJC)	1,833,000	Eb
Universal Fellowship of Metropolitan Community Churches (UFMCC)	171,000	Ed
World Assemblies of God Fellowship (WAGF)	52,220,000	Ca
World Council of Biblical Churches (WCBC)	8,400	Eb
World Evangelical Congregational Fellowship (WECF)	53,900	Ec
World Fellowship of Reformed Churches (WFRC)	1,109,000	Ec
40 other Conservative networks opposed to historic confessions: ABWE,		
BMM, EFMA,GMU, IARPC, IFMA, NTM, UFM, UPC, et alia	12,212,000	Ee

9. Worldwide communions with heterodox christologies

Church of Christ, Scientist	2,500,000	Ec
Church of Jesus Christ of Latter-day Saints (CJCLdS)	12,291,000	Db
International Alliance of Churches of the Truth	800,000	Ed
International Council of Unitarians and Universalists (ICUU)	282,000	Ed
Jehovah's Christian Witnesses (Watch Tower, IBRA, JWs)	16,541,000	Da
Unification Church (Holy Spirit Association for World Christianity)	839,000	Ed
40 other non- or antitrinitarian heterodox communions: IACT, IARF,		
IGAS, INTA, et alia	2,000,000	Ed

10. Unattached denominations with no CWC, no minicommunion,
no claim to be one, no wider communion nor formal relations with
other denominations of similar ecclesiastical tradition, sending
out independent missionaries   206,353,000 Dd

Total combined memberships in 350 CWCs	5,214,662,400	Ab
Doubly-affiliated members (counted in 2 or more CWCs)	-3,404,662,400	
Total individual members in 350 CWCs throughout Christian world	1,810,000,000	Ab

Global Table 4. **Foreign mission personnel sent out by, and received by, 238 countries, 7 continents, and the world.**

The data on Christian foreign mission personnel shown below are arranged as one single large 5-variable column set out in 3 pieces consecutively across the page, listing the world's 238 countries in alphabetical order. The last 11 rows list totals by the 7 continents, and by the 3 missiological worlds (World A = unevangelized world, World B = evangelized but non-Christian world, and World C = Christian world, baptized, affiliated). The final righthand bottom row gives global totals. Within each of the 3 pieces, 5 variables are set out, giving total numbers of foreign mission personnel from all Christian churches and traditions.

1. *Short name of country or (last 11 lines) aggregate*
2. *Citizens of this country working abroad as mission personnel*
3. *Citizens working abroad per million of their home country's affiliated church members*
4. *Aliens from abroad working in this country as mission personnel*
5. *Aliens from abroad working in this country as mission personnel per million of this country's total population*

1 Country	2 MSent	3 MSentPM	4 MRecv	5 MRecvPM
Afghanistan	0	0	55	2
Albania	55	45	840	268
Algeria	20	364	530	16
American Samoa	65	1,262	210	3,237
Andorra	40	669	10	149
Angola	340	24	2,100	132
Anguilla	5	478	10	819
Antarctica	0	0	10	1,894
Antigua	2	31	75	920
Argentina	1,900	54	12,700	328
Armenia	110	44	55	18
Aruba	4	44	15	151
Australia	5,800	454	4,600	228
Austria	2,600	409	1,600	195
Azerbaijan	15	74	110	13
Bahamas	20	72	320	991
Bahrain	5	74	55	76
Bangladesh	30	28	1,100	8
Barbados	10	52	210	779
Belgium	10,800	1,312	2,700	259
Belize	10	45	420	1,557
Belorussia	110	17	530	54
Benin	55	23	630	75
Bermuda	10	195	110	1,714
Bhutan	2	117	210	97
Bolivia	3,000	353	4,400	479
Bosnia-Herzegovina	260	198	580	148
Botswana	85	94	420	238
Bougainville	10	51	110	515
Brazil	21,100	124	26,400	142

1 Country	2 MSent	3 MSentPM	4 MRecv	5 MRecvPM
Britain	19,500	500	15,800	265
British Indian Ocean	5	5,669	10	5,000
British Virgin Is	4	266	10	454
Brunei	2	36	30	80
Bulgaria	110	17	210	27
Burkina Faso	40	16	1,100	83
Burundi	160	25	1,300	172
Cambodia	4	22	320	23
Cameroon	420	51	3,700	227
Canada	17,400	853	8,400	260
Cape Verde	85	176	110	217
Cayman Islands	2	65	20	444
Central African Rep	85	43	1,100	272
Chad	30	15	790	81
Channel Islands	15	154	10	67
Chile	1,800	128	8,400	515
China	5,300	48	4,200	3
Christmas Island	10	33,333	10	6,667
Cocos (Keeling) Is	5	37,037	5	7,813
Colombia	3,700	84	7,400	162
Comoros	2	589	40	59
Congo-Brazzaville	130	44	840	210
Congo-Zaire	1,100	21	15,800	275
Cook Islands	10	591	75	4,177
Costa Rica	740	178	1,500	347
Croatia	320	79	1,600	352
Cuba	20	3	260	23
Cyprus	55	94	210	326
Czech Republic	260	53	1,600	157
Denmark	630	136	1,500	276
Djibouti	5	373	80	101
Dominica	5	67	85	1,077
Dominican Republic	140	17	2,100	236
Ecuador	420	33	3,700	280
Egypt	320	30	1,600	22
El Salvador	210	31	1,500	218
Equatorial Guinea	55	125	320	636
Eritrea	130	63	210	48
Estonia	40	79	160	120
Ethiopia	260	6	2,600	34
Faeroe Islands	55	1,264	30	638
Falkland Islands	20	9,794	10	3,268
Fiji	110	230	630	743
Finland	1,500	332	530	101
France	32,200	781	16,900	279
French Guiana	20	127	210	1,123
French Polynesia	30	141	420	1,637
Gabon	20	18	420	304
Gambia	4	70	180	119
Georgia	65	23	110	25
Germany	28,000	480	10,600	128
Ghana	580	51	2,100	95
Gibraltar	10	428	40	1,433
Greece	420	41	530	48
Greenland	2	51	65	1,142
Grenada	10	101	130	1,263
Guadeloupe	150	352	420	936
Guam	25	164	480	2,830
Guatemala	480	41	3,700	294
Guinea	2	8	110	12
Guinea-Bissau	10	48	200	126

1 Country	*2* MSent	*3* MSentPM	*4* MRecv	*5* MRecvPM
Guyana	10	26	320	426
Haiti	30	4	1,600	188
Holy See	120	156,454	210	268,199
Honduras	210	31	840	117
Hungary	260	29	1,300	129
Iceland	40	145	40	136
India	7,400	108	8,400	8
Indonesia	630	22	6,300	28
Iran	20	54	210	3
Iraq	40	54	85	3
Ireland	9,800	2,658	530	128
Isle of Man	20	389	4	52
Israel	55	287	1,100	164
Italy	33,300	700	12,700	219
Ivory Coast	320	56	1,800	99
Jamaica	43	38	740	279
Japan	840	254	7,900	62
Jordan	15	90	210	37
Kazakhstan	30	15	210	14
Kenya	840	31	6,300	184
Kirgizstan	30	93	55	10
Kiribati	10	109	55	554
Kuwait	10	39	110	41
Laos	5	30	85	14
Latvia	65	42	420	182
Lebanon	210	163	630	176
Lesotho	55	40	690	384
Liberia	75	76	530	161
Libya	5	30	110	19
Liechtenstein	25	838	20	579
Lithuania	230	81	420	122
Luxembourg	130	304	40	86
Macedonia	55	42	160	79
Madagascar	320	35	2,100	113
Malawi	420	50	1,600	124
Malaysia	95	42	1,100	43
Maldives	0	0	10	30
Mali	10	27	630	47
Malta	1,100	2,904	30	75
Marshall Islands	10	175	85	1,372
Martinique	85	228	210	530
Mauritania	0	0	55	18
Mauritius	40	101	320	258
Mayotte	0	0	30	261
Mexico	4,800	47	8,400	78
Micronesia	55	546	510	4,616
Moldavia	110	39	530	126
Monaco	20	669	160	4,539
Mongolia	5	131	420	159
Montserrat	2	469	10	2,228
Morocco	15	133	1,600	51
Mozambique	160	24	3,400	172
Myanmar	260	63	210	4
Namibia	55	33	1,300	640
Nauru	2	204	20	1,467
Nepal	110	116	950	35
Netherlands	10,800	1,162	2,200	135
Netherlands Antilles	20	129	630	3,449
New Caledonia	30	170	320	1,351
New Zealand	2,200	962	3,000	745
Nicaragua	260	50	2,100	383

1	2	3	4	5
Country	MSent	MSentPM	MRecv	MRecvPM
Niger	10	159	480	34
Nigeria	2,600	42	5,600	43
Niue	10	7,536	5	3,460
Norfolk Island	10	7,289	5	2,322
North Korea	2	5	20	1
Northern Cyprus	2	727	40	210
Northern Mariana Is	5	70	130	1,609
Norway	1,900	436	1,100	238
Oman	2	28	40	16
Pakistan	55	14	1,600	10
Palau	10	535	20	1,003
Palestine	260	3,005	1,300	351
Panama	630	229	2,200	681
Papua New Guinea	110	24	3,800	670
Paraguay	480	83	1,300	211
Peru	840	31	7,200	257
Philippines	2,100	29	10,000	120
Pitcairn Islands	1	16,129	1	14,925
Poland	2,600	71	740	19
Portugal	5,300	551	790	75
Puerto Rico	970	259	2,600	657
Qatar	4	46	10	12
Reunion	10	15	250	318
Romania	210	10	1,100	51
Russia	1,100	13	20,100	140
Rwanda	130	19	1,300	144
Sahara	0	0	10	29
Saint Helena	5	1,217	20	4,067
Saint Kitts & Nevis	2	50	40	937
Saint Lucia	4	27	160	995
Saint Pierre & Miquelon	10	1,847	40	6,934
Saint Vincent	2	25	85	714
Samoa	320	1,847	840	4,541
San Marino	6	239	20	711
São Tomé & Príncipe	20	142	110	703
Saudi Arabia	10	8	110	4
Senegal	95	151	1,300	112
Serbia & Montenegro	530	80	1,100	105
Seychelles	15	202	160	1,984
Sierra Leone	10	17	740	134
Singapore	530	854	1,100	254
Slovakia	75	17	1,100	204
Slovenia	160	94	840	427
Solomon Islands	45	104	530	1,109
Somalia	4	68	55	12
Somaliland	0	0	10	3
South Africa	7,400	214	12,700	268
South Korea	15,800	820	3,000	63
Spain	32,200	820	2,600	60
Spanish North Africa	10	111	55	417
Sri Lanka	210	107	1,800	87
Sudan	110	19	740	20
Suriname	25	132	420	935
Svalbard & Jan Mayen	10	5,444	5	1,295
Swaziland	110	169	840	814
Sweden	2,100	350	1,100	122
Switzerland	3,600	593	2,300	317
Syria	160	162	110	6
Taiwan	420	335	3,200	140
Tajikistan	5	51	40	6
Tanzania	320	17	4,800	125

1 Country	2 MSent	3 MSentPM	4 MRecv	5 MRecvPM
Thailand	30	28	2,100	33
Timor	40	50	110	116
Togo	85	33	630	103
Tokelau Islands	5	4,000	10	7,257
Tonga	55	593	420	4,105
Trinidad & Tobago	160	206	530	406
Tunisia	4	80	210	21
Turkey	30	121	530	7
Turkmenistan	2	27	55	11
Turks & Caicos Is	2	94	10	380
Tuvalu	2	231	10	958
Uganda	530	21	2,700	94
Ukraine	420	11	4,400	95
United Arab Emirates	10	23	130	29
USA	115,700	578	35,100	118
Uruguay	630	283	3,200	924
Uzbekistan	5	13	210	8
Vanuatu	10	53	320	1,514
Venezuela	970	39	7,400	277
Viet Nam	840	115	1,300	15
Virgin Is of the US	20	219	160	1,431
Wallis & Futuna Is	2	133	30	1,938
Yemen	2	55	160	8
Zambia	260	28	3,400	291
Zimbabwe	420	54	2,900	223
Africa	18,406	46	95,765	106
Antarctica	0	0	10	1,894
Asia	35,862	105	61,405	16
Europe	203,211	381	111,829	154
Latin America	43,967	85	114,150	203
Northern America	133,122	603	43,715	132
Oceania	8,957	402	16,651	504
World A	745	38	13,750	19
World B	44,511	79	112,020	28
World C	398,269	275	317,755	178
Global Total	**443,525**	**218**	**443,525**	**69**

11

The "Jesus" Film: A Contribution to World Evangelism

Paul A. Eshleman

On Saturday night, August 19, 2000, following an address by Pope John Paul II at the World Youth Day in Rome, the "Jesus" film was viewed by over one million young people. In the preceding four days, 694,000 videocassettes of the film were distributed to young people at eighty-five locations throughout the city.

During the period between Christmas 1999 and Easter 2000, over 700 million people saw telecasts of a special millennial edition of the "Jesus" film. Shown on national television in 122 countries, the film contained tributes from thirty-two world leaders.

And on February 10, 2000, seven-year-old Amber watched the new children's edition of the "Jesus" video in her living room and prayed the prayer at the end to receive Christ as her Savior. The video film was a gift from her new parents, who had just adopted her.

For a million young people in Rome, for the nations of the world, or for a seven-year-old orphan, Jesus and his incomparable Gospel is still the greatest news ever announced to our world. And the way that many have been seeing, hearing, and understanding the message has been through the "Jesus" film, a two-hour documentary outlining Jesus' life and teachings.

Roots of the Project

I began working on this project in 1978. The vision for using a film on the life of Jesus for evangelism first came to Bill Bright, founder and president of Campus Crusade for Christ, in 1945. Over the years he never found a film on Jesus that he could use, nor—until 1978—was it clear how funds could be secured for the production.

In the early 1970s a similar idea about making films based on the Scriptures came to the well-known Hollywood film producer John

Heyman, who produced or funded numerous award-winning and best-selling films (*Saturday Night Fever, The Longest Yard, Black Sunday, Heaven Can Wait, Gandhi,* and others). Heyman had lost dozens of his Jewish relatives in the Holocaust. As he read the Scriptures, he saw in them the basis for our system of law and justice, and indeed for the foundations of our society. He felt that the best thing he could do for the world was to bring these truths to the motion picture screen. With funding secured from investors in his secular projects, Heyman began what he called the Genesis Project. The goal of the project was to portray every scene of the Bible, from Genesis through Revelation, as accurately as possible.

Heyman began with the Book of Genesis. As the characters spoke Hebrew, a voice-over narration in English provided the biblical text verse by verse, without alteration. All the filming was done in the Holy Land, as close as possible to where the original events took place. Costumes were designed according to the drawings found on the pyramids showing the dress of Hebrew slaves. All the cloth used in the film was hand woven. Yemenite Jews were selected as actors because their facial features are thought to have changed little over the millennia.

After Heyman had completed eight fifteen-minute films covering the first twenty chapters of Genesis and two additional films covering chapters 1 and 2 of Luke, one of his consultants encouraged him to seek the assistance of Campus Crusade for Christ in marketing these films to churches. This led, in 1976, to a meeting with Bill Bright. I met Heyman at this time and we struck up a friendship. Then, at Bright's personal request, I was seconded to the Genesis Project offices in New York, where I helped in the distribution of the first episodes of these Bible-teaching films. They were promoted as the New Media Bible.

The Dreams Realized

During 1977 Heyman began thinking about producing feature films on the Bible that could go into commercial theaters. It was hoped that the profits generated would be sufficient to produce the remaining films on Genesis and Luke and then to go on to the Books of Exodus and Acts, and so on through the whole Bible. The decision was made to begin with a feature film on the life of Jesus, with the Gospel of Luke selected as the script basis because it is the most complete in relating the events of Jesus' life.

In August 1978 Columbia Pictures, MCA, Universal, and other

film distributors were approached to provide the financing and theater distribution for the feature film. By the end of August, Warner Brothers had agreed to put up funding for distribution of the film in theaters throughout North America if production funding could be secured elsewhere. At that time Campus Crusade for Christ was holding a weekend conference for a small number of its donors to talk about laying plans for a worldwide evangelization initiative. It was felt that some kind of film on the life of Jesus should be a part of it. Heyman spoke to the group, briefing them about the possibilities of a film on the life of Jesus. At that point Bunker and Caroline Hunt, longtime friends of Bill and Vonette Bright, agreed to guarantee a loan for the production funds.

According to the agreement reached for the film, the Genesis Project undertook to do the production. Campus Crusade for Christ obtained the "missionary" rights for the film in the noncommercial areas of the world, while Warner Brothers was assigned distribution rights in areas of the world where there was a commercial market for the film and funds might be recouped toward production costs.

With the New Media Bible in mind, Heyman proceeded to film all twenty-four chapters of Luke for the New Media Bible. At the same time, and using the same sets, he produced the footage for the "Jesus" film. The difference in the two productions was that in the feature film the actors spoke English and material from the Gospel was selected to fit the length of a feature film, while in the Genesis Project's Book of Luke the actors spoke Aramaic and nothing was omitted.

Warner Brothers released the film in October 1979, and it eventually played in 2,000 theaters in North America. Then it moved to ShowTime, HBO, and the Movie Channel. In the succeeding years most of the international distribution rights for the film were secured by Campus Crusade. In 1981 I returned to the staff of Campus Crusade for Christ, and the Jesus Film Project was launched to handle the translation and distribution of the film internationally. We were charged with raising whatever funding and staffing would be necessary for the effort. Our mission was to show the "Jesus" film to every person in the world in an understandable language and in a setting near where they live.

Two Decades of Progress

Over the last two decades we have seen the "Jesus" film become the most-watched, and the most-translated, film in world history. Because so many denominations and missions use the film, it is impossible to know all that is taking place through its use. The following highlights give an idea of where the film has gone and a sense of its spiritual impact around the world.

- 11 million students saw the film in Russian schools as a result of the CoMission initiative.
- It has been distributed to every member of the parliaments or congresses of several countries, including the Ukraine, New Zealand, and Mongolia.
- When the film was first screened in Mongolia, there were only a few known believers in the entire country. Now the film has been shown in every village of over 250 people, and there are 30,000 believers worshiping in 400 churches.
- Before she died, Mother Teresa asked for it to be shown in all her homes for the dying in Calcutta, India.
- Screenings have been done in over 400,000 villages of India in 51 languages.
- 55 language translations are available to be downloaded from the Internet. The language most requested, after English, is Arabic.
- Since 1999 over 1 million video and audio cassettes of the "Jesus" film have been sent into North Africa.
- In 2000, newspapers in Brazil sold the "Jesus" video as a special promotion to new subscribers. In this way 250,000 videos were distributed during the year.
- Stories of healing are a regular part of reports from the field. As people see Jesus heal people in the film, they have asked God for—and experienced—their own healing.
- Most important, coming from these showings have been over 115,000 new churches where new believers can grow in their faith.

Methods of Distribution

In order to give fullest access to the "Jesus" film, the project has developed a number of delivery systems.

Theater. We prepare 35mm films for release in theaters. When the Soviet Union collapsed, the "Jesus" film was one of the first major films from the West to receive widespread distribution, being shown in more than 2,000 theaters.

Television. National television offers one of the best means of getting the film to the high-rise apartments of the major cities and urban areas.

Personal access. The film is available in a variety of formats for personal use, including videocassette, CD (compact disk), VCD (video compact disk), and DVD (digital versatile disk). In China and South East Asia, VCD is the most popular format, outselling videocassettes 10 to 1. The DVD version of the "Jesus" film includes eight translations of the film on one disk.

16mm film. Though it is no longer a popular format in media-sophisticated countries, 16mm film remains the delivery vehicle of choice for most rural areas of the world. The Jesus Film Project is currently the largest buyer of 16mm projectors in the world.

Audio cassettes. A dramatized 90-minute audio cassette version was originally developed for schools for the blind in South Africa. It has, however, become a popular means of follow-up for the film showings and a wonderful evangelistic tool in its own right. It can be used in rural areas for both evangelism and followup. It is equally effective in certain other areas, where it can be played on car radios as listeners sit in traffic jams in the world's large cities. India produced more than 1 million audiotapes in the first six months of 2000. The United Bible Societies stocks them for nonreaders.

Radio. We have also produced a radio production entitled "The Story of Jesus." It is based on the script, but more narration and new sound effects have been added. Currently, there are 212 audio/radio translations available, with over fifty more in process.

Strengths of the Project

On the human level, many factors help explain why the "Jesus" film has been so well received.

It is based on Scripture. To me, this is the most significant reason why the film has engendered such a wide response. Certainly there have been more exciting portrayals with more expensive sets and stars. But the power of the "Jesus" film is in the script—the Gospel of St. Luke. The film's Jesus speaks no words outside those found in Scripture.

It is translated into every major language. Nothing can compare with the power of the Word of God if it is heard in an understandable language. A mother in India wrote to her son in New York, "Son, I have just seen a film about Jesus. And Jesus speaks Bengali!" It is difficult to overestimate the impact of hearing the Gospel in the language of one's heart. From its inception, those of us involved in the Jesus Film Project have believed that no one should have to learn another language to hear the "greatest story ever told." (The most-dubbed Hollywood effort, *Gone with the Wind*, stopped after thirty-three language translations.)

It relates to the developing world. Many people today still live in a first-century kind of environment. They still fish and farm for a living. Many wear sandals, and a wealthy man is someone who owns an oxcart. These people find Jesus' illustrations extremely relevant; for them, some of the scenes could have been filmed in a nearby village.

It enables churches to be planted quickly. The "Jesus" film has provided a new model for church planting that greatly accelerates the process. In many areas, missionaries are finding that it takes only one showing of the "Jesus" film to identify enough interested new converts to start a new church. Many seminaries and Bible schools regularly send their students out to conduct film showings in order to help them plant a new church by the time they graduate. The "Jesus" film is simply a filter to find the ripe fruit that God has already prepared.

It calls for a decision. Wherever Jesus went, he called men and women to repentance and to follow him. The clear presentation of the Gospel included at the end of the film allows even the most inexperienced workers to give a powerful appeal for men and women to receive Jesus as Savior and Lord.

It contributes to unity in the body of Christ. One of the unexpected blessings coming from the release of the "Jesus" film has been the uniting of the body of Christ in many countries for cooperative showings. Many times we have missed the full impact and potential of John 17:23 ("May they be brought to complete unity to let the world know that you sent me and have loved them even as you have loved me"). Throughout the world, pastors have gathered to discuss plans to show the film or distribute videocassettes to every home. Frequently during these prayer and planning sessions, long-standing grievances have been healed, sins confessed to one another, and relationships healed. It has made me wonder whether loving one another may be God's greatest strategic plan for worldwide evangelism.

The Follow-up Plan

New believers need nurturing in their faith. The Jesus Film Project has developed follow-up strategies to help assure lasting results following film showings. First, members of local churches are trained in advance to help provide follow-up. They meet with those who come forward after the film to pray with them and write down their addresses for future visits.

Second, "New Life" groups are formed to disciple new believers, with elders from local churches leading the groups. Groups will often combine to form new churches.

Third, New Life Training Centers provide 100 hours of instruction for new church leaders in personal evangelism, personal follow-up, principles of starting a discipleship group, how to teach the Scripture, and much more. Half of the course is spent in the field. As a result, by the end of the training course many of the trainees have led people to Christ and have started a Bible study.

Finally, Media Response Centers coordinate follow-up from television and radio presentations of the "Jesus" film, as well as answer responses from the audio and videotape distribution. Every video, audiotape, radio or TV program offers an address where more information can be obtained.

A Worldwide Strategic Plan

The primary plan of the Jesus Film Project is to be a servant to the whole body of Christ. Though the organization itself has grown rapidly, internal growth has never been the objective. Helping everyone, everywhere to see the film has always been paramount. However, we have followed certain key principles to see this goal accomplished.

We seek to build models of film-team evangelism. Because these teams are always made up of nationals, they can demonstrate to believers what is involved in setting up and promoting evangelistic showings and in gathering new believers and serious inquirers into local churches.

Many advantages result from setting up models of ministry

indigenous to each country. First, they provide direct feedback when a strategy is not working so that adjustments can be made. When Americans work with international partners, it is difficult for the international participants to inform American colleagues candidly when something is not effective; they simply quit using the resources. Having a few Jesus Film Project teams in every country allows us to learn lessons that can then be passed on to all users.

A second advantage of such teams is their recommendations on how to give the invitation more effectively. Although an informative five-minute presentation is included at the end of every film, in some cultures audiences will not watch it after the film has ended. In those places, the workers might pause the film at the crucifixion scene, explain that Jesus died for everyone, and give an opportunity for response right then. The process of finding out who is interested in knowing more is carried out in a variety of ways, depending on the culture and the openness of the country.

A third area of feedback from the teams is recommendations on how the film should be introduced or any slight variations that should be made. On the basis of such recommendations we have produced over thirty-five versions of the film for different audiences in order to gain a better hearing for the message. For example, we have editions with a Muslim-sensitive introduction, others with Asian introductions on why a Hindu or Buddhist should learn about Jesus, a Tibetan version, a closed-caption/sign language edition, a "World Cup" edition (introductory testimonies of nine soccer players), and a "More Than Gold" edition (testimonies of ten Olympic athletes).

We seek to establish ministry partnerships. We want the film showings to benefit partnering churches and mission agencies. These and other organizations use the film for a variety of objectives, including church planting, Christian education, work among the preliterate, Vacation Bible Schools, summer camps, short-term mission trips, community saturation projects, premarital counseling classes, and English as a Second Language classes.

The biggest users of the "Jesus" film so far are the Church of the Nazarene, the Southern Baptist International Mission Board, World Vision, Operation Mobilization, and the Roman Catholic Church. The great advantage of having many partners and distributors is that costs are widely shared. The disadvantage of trying to involve partners is that they usually have a very defined geographic target area and are not always committed to widespread coverage strategies.

We seek to track progress. One of our core goals is to preach the Gospel where Christ is not known (Rom. 15:20). Since the beginning of the project, we have tried to capture statistically how many people have seen the film by country and language, and what the results have been. The primary purpose of this exercise has always been to try to determine who has not seen the film yet—and continually to adjust strategic plans toward unreached areas.

As of March 1, 2002, our statistics show that, since 1979

- 4,937,942,748 people have seen the "Jesus" film in 236 countries (shown on TV in 174 of these countries);
- 729 languages now have translations of the "Jesus" film (translations are in progress in an additional 253 languages; a new translation is completed every three days);
- 152,176,072 decisions for Christ have been indicated;
- 34,357,719 "Jesus" film videocassettes have been distributed, plus 54,640 DVDs, 1,247,666 VCDs, 14,729 film prints (8mm, 16mm, and 35mm), 8,716,340 cassettes of "The Story of Jesus" audio version, and 618,103 videocassettes of "The Story of Jesus for Children";
- 2,797 full-time "Jesus" film teams, with 6,220 total workers, are operating in 108 countries;
- 1,524 denominations and mission agencies are working in partnership with the Jesus Film Project.

Difficulties and Challenges

The "Jesus" film is simply a tool. It has limitations, and it may not be equally effective in every situation. However, because it contains the powerful words of Scripture, there are almost always *some* results when it is presented properly. Over the years we have faced a long list of challenges in the translation and distribution of the film.

Translation challenges. The translation and dubbing must be as close to perfect as possible, which means that we often must redub portions of the film. For example, in the initial film edition of Zhuang, a language group in China, our translation of "angels" was actually "fairies." We fixed the problem. In Kinyarwanda (Rwanda), Mary asked, "Am I a virgin?" instead of stating, "I am a virgin." We changed it. In Ilocano (Philippines), when the translators needed a word for "prostitute," they used a term comparable to "hooker." Although it was good contemporary Illocano, it offended local pastors, and they refused to show the film. We changed the word.

Missionaries and local churches sometimes fight to retain "Christian" words, which may lessen the impact of the film with nonbelievers. One disputed word is the name for Jesus, which in Muslim countries has been translated either "Yesu" (often favored by Christians) or "Isa" (the Arabic usage). We continually push for "Isa" because we are trying to reach Muslims. Some Christians have refused to show the film with this translation.

Finally, wrong voices or accents are sometimes selected. In many cultures around the world, Jesus is expected to have the accent of the highest caste or class. If a voice with a low-class accent is used, the viewing audience is limited. Sometimes we have faced the problem of communicating to warring tribes that speak the same language but with slightly different accents. Which tribal voice do you choose for Jesus?

Over the past twenty-one years the Jesus Film Project has spent more than $2 million to correct translation and dubbing errors and problems.

Distribution challenges. Without a doubt, the biggest distribution challenges occur in media-sophisticated urban areas, where residents have lots of media to choose from. There the delivery system of the film must be much different. Strategies of inviting nonbelievers to a church or hall are largely ineffective. Outdoor showings on a screen are inappropriate. For the urban, media-sophisticated areas there are at least four options: television broadcast on secular channels, house-to-house or mail distribution of videocassettes, secular radio station broadcasts, or home showings to friends and neighbors.

A different distribution challenge is urban areas where the church is small and there is no access to radio or TV, such as in Saudi Arabia, North Korea, or Algeria. Here the distribution of the film is limited to distribution by short-term "tourists," radio broadcasts from the outside, port projects, and contact with vacationers when they are outside their countries.

A final problem in distribution involves disputes among Christian confessions as to who may show the film. The Jesus Film Project has never tried to prevent anyone from buying or showing a videocassette, which has caused some difficulty in countries where two different Christian groups (often Catholics and Protestants, or charismatics and noncharismatics) have the film. Each may be afraid of losing people to the other confession or tradition. We have been accused of selling "arms" to both sides. Our response is that the "Jesus" film is simply the Word of God on film. Every person should have access to God's truth.

Challenges in follow-up and discipleship. Adequate preparation must be made to immediately follow up those who express interest after seeing the "Jesus" film. The groups that are disappointed in showing the film are those groups that do not prepare for the discipleship process. We are not in the entertainment business but are attempting to find those whom God has prepared and help them take the next step, which is to become part of a local body of believers. In order to do this, local believers must be prepared in advance, in at least the following ways:

- Counselors must be trained separately for the men, women, and children who will respond. It is not effective to try to counsel them together.
- There must be a clear, effective invitation given at the end of the film.
- There must be a sufficiently lighted area available after the showing to meet with interested people, distribute literature, review the gospel presentation, and write down addresses for further contact.
- People must be prepared to do house visits where questions can be answered and relationships begun.
- A follow-up group must be established in a neutral location.
- Before the film is shown, someone must commit to lead the group of inquirers. This person is usually an elder from the church sponsoring the showing.

All these steps require people and time. Without a commitment in advance to these steps, we have found that church-planting efforts will not be effective.

Lack of the incarnational message. TV and radio broadcasts can help identify those with a genuine interest in the Christian Gospel. But that is only the first step toward their eventual involvement in the "family." There needs to be an incarnational witness. Distribution of videos from neighbor to neighbor or friend to friend is the most successful. The most effective film showings are those where interested inquirers are able to interact with "live" believers who answer questions and form the beginning of an ongoing relationship. Many times it is the life of Jesus seen in the believer that produces the motivation to receive Christ.

Our Vision for the Future

Initially, our goal was to prepare a film translation for every language with at least I million speakers (which, in 1981, we thought meant 163 languages). Our current goal is much broader, as we now aim to include every language spoken by as few as 50,000 people—in all, 1,813 languages—which will allow 97.8 percent of the world's population to hear the message in their first language. Most of the remaining people will be able to understand the presentation via a trade language.

As the Jesus Film Project moves ahead in the new millennium, I am committed to see it continue to serve the body of Christ in every way possible. Currently, we have the following specific goals:

- Continue to make the film available in the formats needed for new technology (for example, DVD and streaming on the Internet).
- Do more to equip churches, denominations, and organizations to use the "Jesus" film effectively in church planting.
- Prepare more written, video, and audio materials for the follow-up of new believers.
- Develop materials using the dramatized audio version of the "Jesus" film for follow-up after film showings. Such materials can powerfully reinforce what people see in the film and can engage family members and friends not present at the film showing.
- Translate all materials for "The Story of Jesus for Children." By 2010 at least 50 percent of the world will be under the age of eighteen, and we want to be at the forefront in reaching these young people.

Index